I'M AT A LOSS FOR WORDS

What to Say When You Don't Know What to Say

Cynthia MacGregor

Adams Media Corporation
Avon, Massachusetts

Published by
Adams Media Corporation
57 Littlefield Street, Avon, MA 02322 U.S.A.
www.adamsmedia.com

ISBN: 1-58062-655-6

Printed in Canada.

J I H G F E D C B A

Library of Congress Cataloging-in-Publication Data
MacGregor, Cynthia.
    I'm at a loss for words : what to say when you don't know what
to say / by Cynthia MacGregor.
        p.   cm.
    ISBN 1-58062-655-6
    1. Interpersonal communication. 2. Etiquette. I. Title
P94.7 .M33 2002
395—dc21 2001056156

This publication is designed to provide accurate and authoritative information
with regard to the subject matter covered. It is sold with the understanding that
the publisher is not engaged in rendering legal, accounting, or other professional advice. If legal advice or other expert assistance is required, the services
of a competent professional person should be sought.
                        —From a *Declaration of Principles* jointly adopted
                            by a Committee of the American Bar Association
                            and a Committee of Publishers and Associations

This book is available at quantity discounts for bulk purchases.
For information, call 1-800-872-5627.

Contents

Confrontation   42

Apologies/Excuses/Mending Fences   94

Delicate Situations   104

Invitations/Announcements   107

Part Two: Personal Business

Resignation/Dismissal   112

Recommendations   114

Soliciting/Fundraising/Fee Adjusting   117

Complaints/Rejections   122

Advertisements   130

Endorsements/Requests 135

Letters of Thanks 139

Correspondence with Publishers 143

Communicating with Your Landlord
or Service Provider by Letter 146

Where There's a Will . . . 150

Part Three: Strictly Business

Dismissal/Resignation   156

Job Seeking/Hiring   161

Collections/Payments/Price Quotes   170

Customer Relations   190

Rental Space 202

Politics 205

Part Four: Speeches and Toasts

Introduction

It happens to the best of us, even to those who are well spoken. We find ourselves unable to put into words precisely what it is we want to say. The words we want may be needed for a letter, a conversation, or a speech. The occasion may be strictly personal, personal business, or strictly business.

We may be looking for the right thing to say for a sad occasion. Perhaps we need to compose a condolence note or deliver a eulogy.

We may be looking for the words that will serve us best in an awkward or unpleasant situation, such as quitting a job or firing an employee.

Circumstances sometimes require us to select our words with the greatest possible care. For example, consider what you might do if you suspected someone—a friend, a housekeeper, or a recent houseguest—of stealing from you. You need to find a tactful way of asking for your property back. Or perhaps you lent someone an item or some money, and it hasn't been returned or repaid. You need to talk to that person or write to him or her to request—or demand—repayment. Few of us enjoy confrontation, and not knowing quite how to frame what we need to say makes the confrontation even more unpleasant.

That's where this book can help. It can't give you a dose of courage, but it *can*—and will—help you find the right words to say. And if you know how to say what you want or need to say, it makes saying it that much easier . . . whether you're saying it face-to-face, by phone, by e-mail, by old-fashioned postal correspondence, or in some form of a speech.

A speech? Yes, a speech. Even though few of us will ever have to give an acceptance speech on winning an Oscar, Emmy, Tony, or Grammy, you may be expected to say a few words on other social occasions: if your civic club names you Man or Woman of the Year, if you're honored by the PTA, if you're the outgoing president of your club and are expected to welcome the incoming president, or if you're at a wedding, "special" birthday party, or similar festive event and are asked to make a toast.

So whether your need is for business or personal communication, this book can help when you're trying to find the right words for those everyday situations: a thank-you note for a gift you didn't like, a resume when your experience is pretty thin, a letter of complaint about a malfunctioning appliance, a letter of recommendation, or a little chat with that contentious neighbor whose unkempt yard is hurting your property values.

You don't know what to say? That's all right . . . now you know where to look. And from now on, that's 90 percent of what you need to know.

PART ONE
Strictly Personal

Thanks/Compliments/ Praise/Good News

Notes: When writing a thank-you letter, remember that if the gift came by mail, delivery service, or any means other than being handed to you by the giver, one reason for the note is simply to let the giver know the gift has arrived. The other reason, of course, is to offer thanks for the gift. But keep in mind that in all but the most informal situations, you should send a thank-you letter, even for those gifts that were given in person.

When is it acceptable to omit sending a thank-you letter? A good rule of thumb is that you may skip the note if the gift was handed to you in person and was (1) nominal, such as a small hostess gift like a plant or a box of candy, or (2) from a close friend with whom you're generally informal. In most other cases, a note is appropriate. If you're in doubt, send a note. Better to err on the side of being too polite.

What should you say? You can't just write, "Dear Aunt Ruth, Thank you for the sweater. Love, Lee." If Aunt Ruth does not live in your vicinity, you can always combine the thank-you note with a friendly letter and tell her your latest news—whatever items are appropriate to her. Ask about her family or friends or both, and whatever in her life it's appropriate to inquire about.

Of course, the more good things you can say about the gift, the better. Do you think it looks perfect in your house or on you? Does it solve a problem or satisfy a need? Does it fit you wonderfully or replace something you've lost, broken, or otherwise no longer have? Say so. Is it exactly what you wanted or needed? Say so. Does the gift reflect the giver's thoughtfulness or knowledge of what you enjoy? Say so.

Did the giver send the gift at some time other than a traditional gift-giving occasion? Thank her for thinking of you when it wasn't even a holiday, your birthday, or your anniversary.

Wrap the letter up with a repeat "Thank you," and sign it and send it. Simple? Simple! ✎

Thank-you letter to a casual, local acquaintance

Dear Pat,

Thank you so much for the book. You know I enjoy mysteries, and since I haven't read this one yet, it was a great choice. I am looking forward to reading it. I have never read anything by *[author]* before and look forward to discovering an author who is new to me. Who knows? This one may become my latest favorite!

I hope this note finds you well, as I am. Work is the same, and there is nothing much new in my personal life since we talked last, so there's little to report. What's going on in your world? How about getting together for dinner some time soon? Call me and we'll make a plan!

Again, thanks for the gift. It was an excellent choice. And, of course, thanks for thinking of me.

Sincerely,

Thank-you letter to a relative who lives at a distance

Dear Uncle Bob,

Thank you so much for the assortment of fishing gear. It's great! I'm really looking forward to getting out to the lake and bringing the new lures and stuff with me. Bet I catch more fish with your help!

How have you been? How is Aunt Nancy? How's the rest of the family? We're all fine here. Mom and Dad are doing great. They moved into their new home last month, but I suppose they've already told you about that, so I'll skip the details. Work is . . . well, work.

What's left to say? I'm feeling fine, all is well, and I can't wait until my next day with those fish, now that I have all the neat stuff you sent! You do know me and what I enjoy, don't you?

Well, thanks again for a really great gift!

Love,

Thank-you letter for a monetary gift

Dear Ms. Powers,

Thank you so much for the check. That was very generous of you! I was tickled that you remembered my birthday again—you never forget!—and I was certainly pleased at your generosity.

I plan to use your gift to buy myself a hunter green pullover sweater that I've had my eye on for several months now. I'm sure no one else will give me exactly the sweater I've been wanting! But with your generous gift, I will purchase it. So thank you for, in essence, giving me just exactly what I wanted.

Once again, thank you for both your generosity and your thoughtfulness. I will think of you whenever I wear that sweater—and I will wear it often, I assure you.

Sincerely,

Thank-you letter for an inappropriate gift

Notes: When you're writing to thank someone for a gift you don't care for—even a gift you thoroughly despise—you can always find something good to say about it. You may not want to lie and say you love it . . . and you don't have to. (You don't want to encourage the giver to give you something similar next year, do you?) But you can still find something positive to say about the gift.

If it's clothing, is it your color, although not your style? Is it cut in your style, even though the pattern of the cloth isn't to your liking? Is it a cheerful color? Is it a perfect fit? Is it very trendy or classic?

Perhaps it's not clothing. Is it an item you've never received before? Say that nobody else has ever given you a *[fill in the blank]*, and it certainly reflects creative thinking on the part of the giver. Perhaps it's a brand of perfume or aftershave that you can honestly describe as extravagant, or one that makes a bold statement, smells distinctive, or is unique among the scents worn by your friends.

Maybe it's a CD or tape of music you can't stand. Can you say it's lively, cheerful, distinctive, or different? At least you can say no one else gave you the same gift!

Do you get the idea? Find something to say that's positive, that's appreciative, that sounds as though you really think the gift is great . . . even if you absolutely can't stand it! Remember that the giver was thoughtful enough to remember you and went to the trouble of picking out the gift, so honor those good intentions.

If you don't say you love it, you're not lying. You're just pointing out the gift's good points . . . and every gift has *some* good points, even if it's only that you don't have anything else like it.

And, again, you can fill out the rest of the note with social chitchat. The entire letter doesn't have to be about the gift. Depending on who the giver is, you can find other things to talk about to make the note seem sufficiently long—family news, in the case of a relative who lives at a distance, chitchat about yourself and your job or school, and perhaps, for someone who lives nearby, the suggestion that you get together soon.

Letter thanking your host for his hospitality

Dear Ralph,

What can I say? You and Eileen are the perfect hosts! It was a wonderful weekend, made more so by your charming hospitality. The beach house is marvelous, your cooking is out of this world, and the proverbial good time was had by all. Andrew and I had a perfect time, and we thank you deeply.

We look forward to having you over for dinner soon. It won't begin to pay you back for your hospitality this weekend, but at least it will give us a chance to enjoy the pleasure of your company again.

Sincerely,

Letter praising an author's work

Dear Ms. Smith,

I have just finished reading your latest book, *[title],* and I felt I had to let you know how *[choose one or more, or substitute other more appropriate adjective(s)]* meaningful/true/relevant/helpful/courageous I found your writing to be.

[Insert paragraph if relevant]

Your book was of particular significance to me because *[give reason].*

I'm sure your book has occasioned many letters of praise. I don't expect an answer, but I wanted to let you know what an impact *[title]* had on me.

I eagerly await the publication of your next book!

Sincerely,

Letter acknowledging the return of a borrowed item

Dear Helen,

Just wanted to let you know the package arrived safely and the book is back with me. I appreciate your taking such good care of it, especially knowing how irreplaceable it is. I don't usually let this book out of my house, as I told you, but I knew you would take good care of it and return it in good condition. I was mainly concerned about a mail mishap. I hope you enjoyed it.

I also hope this letter finds you and your family healthy and happy and work going well.

Sincerely,

Letter thanking a clergyperson for officiating at a joyous occasion

Dear Father/Rabbi/Cantor/Reverend *[name]*,

We just wanted to thank you for officiating at *[name]*'s *[occasion]*. You helped make the ceremony very special, and we appreciate your major contribution to this joyous/important/happy occasion.

Again, our deep thanks.

Gratefully,

Letter thanking a clergyperson for officiating at a funeral

Dear Reverend/Father/Rabbi/Cantor *[name]*,

Thank you so much for your help at this difficult time. Your well-thought-out words and your manner helped ease the pain at *[name]*'s funeral, and I am deeply grateful. I may not have said as much to you at the funeral—certainly it was a difficult time—but I wanted you to know how much your being there, and what you said, meant to me.

With much appreciation,

General letter of congratulations

Dear Will,

Congratulations! I was so glad to hear the news/read the article in the paper. You certainly deserved the honor/award/promotion.

[Or] You must be very proud of your son/daughter/*[other]*.

[Or] What an accomplishment!/What a feather in your cap.

Sincerely,

Letter of thanks to a hairdresser

Dear Kevin,

Thank you for the marvelous job you did in making my hair look extra-special for my sister's wedding. I felt so pretty as a result, I was afraid I would outshine the bride! You're a magician, and I really wanted to say "Thanks!"

Sincerely,

Letter asking a hostess to share a recipe

Dear Allison,

Thank you once again for having me over to dinner on Thursday. As I said at the time, everything was simply scrumptious. The chicken in particular was absolutely delicious, which is the point of this letter. I would love to have the recipe. If it is not an old family secret, would you mind sharing it with me? Perhaps you could take a minute to write it down or photocopy it? If that's a bother, maybe you could just read it to me over the phone. I'd really appreciate it! Thanks so much.

Sincerely,

Letter asking a restaurant to share a recipe

Good morning,

I had the pleasure of having dinner at your restaurant last night. I enjoyed my meal enormously, as did my dinner companions, but the dish that stands out in my mind was the house special, your chicken à la Vittorio. I don't have the words to describe how delicious it was.

Although nothing can take the place of dining out—the ambience, the variety of good foods, and, of course, the luxury of not having to cook or clean up—I would love to be able to re-create that chicken dish in my own kitchen. Is there any chance you would be willing to share the recipe?

I am enclosing a self-addressed stamped envelope, and I hope you will be kind enough to mail a copy of that recipe to me in it.

With thanks in advance,

Letter of thanks to a dinner host

Dear Dale,

What a delicious dinner! Thank you so much for inviting me! *[Add if appropriate.]* And your other guests were so interesting!

The food was divine . . . but I'd expect that from you. And the company was marvelous as always. I promise to have you over for dinner soon. It may not equal the dinner you served, but we'll have a good time. I certainly enjoyed myself at your house on Saturday! Thanks again.

All the best,

Letter congratulating someone on a forthcoming wedding

Dear Lorna,

What wonderful news! I am so happy for you! I was so pleased to hear/read of your engagement, and you know I wish you and *[fiancé's name]* all happiness in the years ahead.

You'll be a beautiful, radiant bride; may your married life be just as beautiful, and may the happiness you feel as you walk down the aisle continue to glow in your heart throughout your marriage.

Warmly,

Letter of congratulations
on a milestone birthday

Dear Ms. Bartlett,

Congratulations on reaching such a milestone . . . it couldn't be happening to a nicer person! Reaching this point in your life is certainly cause for celebration, but you should be especially proud of the *way* you have attained it. I think that being the *[use any or all of the following adjectives as applicable, or others you may think of]* nice/intelligent/respected/caring person you are is *really* something to be proud of.

I look forward to congratulating you on your next milestone!

Sincerely,

Letter of congratulations to someone you've been out of touch with

Dear Audrey,

I was so pleased to hear the good news. My sincere congratulations! Although we haven't been in touch in ages, you're still in my thoughts. So when I hear that something good has happened to you, I'm extremely pleased. When word reached me of your marriage, I was delighted.

May this be just one of many happy events and circumstances in your life. I wish you and your new husband much happiness, good health, and whatever else you wish for yourselves.

Sincerely,

Sympathy/Condolence

Notes: Condolence notes are probably the hardest messages to write. Fortunately, they need not be lengthy. You should express how sorry you are to have learned of the death. If you knew the person who died, say something positive about him or her. You may want to recount a time you spent together, a good memory that the bereaved will enjoy as well. Then try to find something comforting to say: perhaps that you know the mourner will always treasure the memories of the deceased person, or that he will be comforted by his many friends who are rallying in sympathy.

You can close the note by urging the mourner to call on you if you can be of any help, or you can say that your prayers or thoughts are with the family.

If there is anything practical that you can think of to do—cook a dinner, pick up groceries—you can offer to do so. Say that you are sure she will be swamped with calls, so you will wait a week to call, but she is not to hesitate to call if you can help in any way.

Letter of condolence

Dear Kathryn,

I was so saddened to hear of your loss. I know how close you were to your mother, and I'm sure you'll miss her very much. But at least, when you remember her, you'll have a treasure of wonderful memories. After a while, Kathryn, when the initial hurt dies down, those memories will bring a glow to your heart. I know your mother touched the lives of many people, and everyone who knew her is a little poorer now because of her death.

I hope you know how many people are holding you in their hearts and wishing you well. My wish for you is that the sharp edge of grief heals over soon, leaving you with the comfort of warm memories.

Sincerely,

Notes: Some people tend to use poetic or flowery language when writing condolence notes. If you're not comfortable with the language in the previous letter, you can certainly say the same thing in simpler words.

Face-to-face condolence

Notes: Many people are uncomfortable with the word "death." And it certainly lacks a certain suavity to say, "I'm sorry your mother died." What you *will* say depends on how well you know the bereaved, what your relationship is to her, and what her relationship was to the person who died.

You can say, "At least she's not suffering any longer." Don't say, "She was suffering so . . . it's all for the better."

- "Hi. How are you? I was sorry to hear about Ed. He was a good guy. . . . We're all going to miss him. . . . How are you holding up? . . . What can I do for you . . . have you over for dinner . . . come and keep you company?"
- "Listen, usually people make a fuss in the first week or two, but I know the pain doesn't go away that quickly. How about coming over to dinner in two or three weeks? You're probably deluged with visitors now, but I bet you'll want company by then."
- "You're looking well. I'm glad to see that! Well, let me know if you need company, a shoulder, some practical help . . . whatever." 🖊

Visiting a seriously ill friend

"How are you holding up, John? Is there anything I can do for you to make you more comfortable?"

[If the visit is at the friend's house, rather than at a hospital or other health facility] "May I do anything around the house for you? I'd be happy to do any little task you might want done.

"Is there anything you want me to bring the next time I visit? A book or something?"

[And then segue into chitchat; tell the friend what's going on in your life. If he speaks of not getting better, or of dying, and you know either of these outcomes is the prognosis, don't say, "Oh, don't be silly," or "Don't be gloomy." Let him face facts and accept reality. Acceptance is a natural stage in the process. You can best help your friend by letting him talk, not by going into denial.]

Conversation with a friend whose relative is terminally ill

"Hey, Greg! Good to see you, buddy. How's it going?

"How's Kayleen doing? What a shocker! Is there anything I can do to help? I can do something practical, like run an errand so you can stay home with her, or I can just listen while you vent. Or I can come over one evening and play cards and give you something else to think about for a while. What do you say?

"Well, remember you've got friends who want to help. Just let me know when.

"Hey, how 'bout this weird weather/that last election/the World Series/the Super Bowl/the Stanley Cup!"

Conversation with someone whose relative has died

"Hi, Marsha. How are you managing?

"I still can't believe it about your dad. And while you're still grieving, you've got to deal with all the legalities and paperwork. Are you coping with all that stuff? Is there any way I can be of help? Don't hesitate to let me know if you need a ride somewhere when you're not up to driving, or just want company, or . . . well, whatever.

"How are the kids handling it? Are they okay?

"Listen, now that most people are done paying condolence calls, how about coming over for dinner one of these nights? Is there a night this week or next that looks good for you?"

Acknowledging the birthday or anniversary of someone who has recently died

"Hi, Pat? How are you? I'm calling because . . . Well, I know today would have been Lee's birthday, so I thought you might want someone to talk to. You want to have lunch this afternoon? Or would dinner tonight be better? You name it."

Letter expressing regret when someone has lost a competition

Dear Pat,

I'm so sorry that you didn't win. What rotten luck! But I still want to congratulate you. You *should* have won . . . you worked hard and you deserved it! So congratulations on a great performance . . . and better luck next time!

Sincerely,

Explaining a death to your young children

Notes: If your kids have already experienced the death of a pet, they have some conception of death. You can start out with "Remember when King died last year?" and then explain that Mr. Woodrow next door has died . . . or Grandpa, or whoever. Ask them if they have any questions. Answer their questions honestly.

If this is their first experience with death, the explanation will be more difficult. I like using the analogy that our bodies are like a pair of sneakers . . . they wear out eventually. And that when someone gets real old, his or her body wears out so badly that it stops working too.

If the person who died *wasn't* very old, you'll have to explain that sometimes people wear out when they get very sick, but you need to explain that the kinds of illnesses that people die from are not like the colds, chicken pox, and other things your kids are likely to get. Otherwise, the next time your child gets a stomach bug, he might think he's going to die!

Of course, if you believe in an afterlife, you can tell the kids that Mr. Woodrow has gone to heaven to live with God and the angels. This belief should provide some comfort. Ask them if they have any questions. They may ask, "Will he be back to visit for Christmas?" or "How can I go see him?" Let them raise these questions. Don't anticipate their questions, because you may end up giving them more information than they can absorb.

If you can't handle this conversation reasonably comfortably, you have a couple of other options:

- If you're a member of a church, synagogue, or mosque, and your personal beliefs are consistent with your religion's teachings, you can ask your priest, minister, rabbi, cantor, or imam to talk to your children and explain death to them. Although it's far better for your children to learn about death from you, learning from a respected leader—as long as he or she shows the proper understanding and respects your children's feelings—is better than ignoring their questions and not acknowledging their feelings and fears.

- You can also buy a book on the subject and read it to your children. Let the author's words do the explaining while your voice provides the comfort and familiarity that they need for reassurance. Put your arm around your children, or sit with them beside you or in your lap, for the reassurance of a physical touch.

When you finish reading the book, ask your children if they have questions or if they understood what the book said. Then answer any further questions and reassure any fears. Death is a complicated subject and, let's face it, a scary one. Now is not the time to say, "See what can happen if you don't wear your helmet when you ride your bike," or "This is why it's so important to look both ways before you cross the street." Don't frighten them. Do answer any questions as honestly as you can. If they seem scared or upset, it doesn't mean you've done a bad job of explaining death; it's a natural reaction for some kids to be scared and for other kids to hop off your lap and abruptly say, "Okay. May I go outside and play now?" even though you've just explained that Grandpa Bob has died and won't be around anymore.

Of course, if you see that, subsequent to Grandpa's death, or the neighbor's, your children are having bad dreams, suddenly refusing to go to bed at night, clinging to you unduly, or in some other way showing signs of having been adversely affected, and if these behaviors don't disappear quickly, you may want to take them to see a psychologist or other counselor. ✐

Conversation with a woman
who has just suffered a miscarriage

"Hi. How are you feeling? I heard about your loss, and I want you to know you have my sympathy. How are you both coping?"

Notes: Don't say, "You can always try again." That sentiment trivializes the miscarriage—a loss of what was, in their minds, already a baby, a future person, perhaps even already named.

Letter of condolence to a couple who has just suffered a miscarriage

Dear Susan and John,

I was very sorry to hear of your loss. I know how difficult this time must be for you—a death in the family, the loss of your baby, the loss of a dream for the future. Better days are ahead, I'm sure. In the meanwhile, if there's anything I can do or any way I can be of help or comfort, please let me know. Call if you just want to talk. (And if you don't, I understand that, too.)

Sincerely,

Notes: You are acknowledging the fact that the miscarriage represents, for them, a death and the loss of a family member, not just a fetus. And, again, do *not* say, "You can always try again."

Telling your young child his pet has died

Notes: If your children already have some under-standing of death—from a previous pet's death or the death of a family member or neighbor, for instance—then you don't have to explain the concept, just tell them of this pet's death. (For more help with explaining death to children, see page 27.) Be sure to explain, though, that pets don't live as long as people. Otherwise they may think that if King, age ten, has died, they may be dying soon, too.)

If you believe in an afterlife, you can tell them King has gone to heaven. Certainly if there is a heaven, dogs and cats are welcome there!

But how do you actually break the news? Be straightforward. Start with a sentence or two of preparatory cushioning, and be sure either to put your arm around them or to sit them on your lap.

If King was run over and wasn't under their care at the time, try "You know how I've always warned you not to run into the street?" *[Or]* "You know how I've always told you not to let King run into the street?"

If King was old, you can start by pointing that out, and then go into the worn-out sneakers analogy.

If King was very sick, you can start by saying that although King wasn't able to get better from his illness, at least he's not hurting anymore.

If neither one fits, the cushion just might be, "I have some very sad news to tell you. Come here and snuggle with me."

Then say, "I'm sorry, but King died this morning. He was too sick to get better," or whatever fits the situation. Again, if it was an illness, make sure the kids understand this isn't something that's likely to happen to them!

If the kids want a funeral and/or a backyard burial (assuming that you have a backyard), let them have it. It may give them some comfort—and a sense of closure. If they ask for a new dog, and there's no reason not to agree, go along with the request. But don't say, "Don't cry—I'll get you another dog." Don't make King's death so trivial that a new dog is the total answer to grief. ✐

Telling your young child
you are getting divorced

Notes: The most important thing with young children is to reassure them that the divorce (or separation) is not the result of anything they did wrong. Small children often think that Daddy (or Mommy) is leaving because *they—the kids—*were bad. The next most important thing is to reassure them that even if the two of you no longer love each other, you both will never stop loving them. And the last thing is to assure them that they will still get to see both of you. (Even if one parent is moving out of town, he [or she] will be back for visits or the kids will be going on periodic airplane rides.) ✎

"Sometimes grownups can't get along. Sometimes they even stop loving each other. Mommies and Daddies will always love their kids. The kind of love parents have for their kids never stops. But sometimes parents stop loving each other. *[Or]* Sometimes, even though they still love each other, parents fight so badly with each other that it's better if they don't live together.

"Daddy and I are getting something called a divorce. That means we won't be married anymore.

We won't be living together anymore.

"There are some things you need to understand. Pay attention—this is very important. First of all, we both still love you and we always will. Second, this is not because of anything you did, and there's nothing you can do to change it. And last, you'll still get to see both of us. Daddy won't live here anymore, but you'll get to see him, probably every other weekend and once during the week. That still has to be worked out yet, though. But however often it works out to be, you *will* still see him.

"I know this isn't happy news, and I'm sorry it will be hard for you, but you can't change it.

"Do you have any questions?"

Notes: If you don't feel up to the challenge of explaining divorce to your young child, Fred Rogers (TV's "Mister Rogers") has written a book for little ones called *Let's Talk about It: Divorce.* Read the book to your child while you snuggle with him, then ask him if he has any questions.

He will undoubtedly have questions after the initial discussion. If he seems to need professional help to cope with the divorce, don't view this as indicating a failure on your part to explain it well. ✐

Telling your older child
you are getting divorced

"You probably know your dad and I haven't been getting along as well as we'd like. It's just not going to work out, and we're going to get a divorce. I know you're upset, and I'm sorry. It's really better this way, though, for all of us.

"Dad's going to look for an apartment somewhere nearby, so it'll be easy for you to visit him. If the judge approves, Dad and I have agreed on his seeing you three weekends every month and one night during the week. Dad will have you all summer, too.

"Do you have any questions, honey?"

Notes: For kids this age—upper elementary school and junior high school—who know what divorce is but will still need reassurance as well as the answers to lots of questions, you might want to buy a book such as the one I've written, *The Divorce Helpbook for Kids.*

But don't just give your child the book and turn her loose. Offer a hug with the book; give her some solid information (not just "Daddy and I are getting divorced—here's a book to help you"), and emphasize that you're there to answer any questions that aren't too private.

"Why are you and Daddy getting divorced?" may be a question you don't want to answer. It's one thing if the child has heard many arguments escalating over time, and you can peg your answer to that. However, if your husband has announced that he is leaving you for another woman, or you've asked him to leave because you caught him in bed with a coworker, or if he's just come out of the closet as gay, it's better to simply say it's a grown-up matter and a private one between you and Daddy. The important thing is that she understands it's not because of anything she did. Even at this age, some children take the blame onto themselves.

There are bound to be questions that go beyond what any book explains. Answer them as forthrightly as you can, or as you feel is appropriate to your child's age and to the circumstances of your divorce.

And, as with younger children, if your child seems to need (or asks for) a few sessions with a professional counselor, by all means let her have that help . . . and don't take it as a signal that your explanation was in any way faulty or lacking. ✎

Talking to a friend whose marriage or relationship has ended

"Hi, Tom. I haven't seen you in a few days. Listen, bad news sure travels fast around here. I heard you're on your own. I'm not asking for details—they're none of my business—but if you *do* want to talk, I'm available.

"Meanwhile, if you'd like to come over for dinner Tuesday, that would be great. We can have dinner, and then maybe we could rent a movie or play cards. What do you say? Sound good?"

Talking to a bride whose wedding has been called off

"I won't ask questions that are none of my business, but if you need a shoulder or just want to talk, I'm here. Meanwhile, I'm sorry that things didn't work out the way you'd hoped. I sure hope something much more wonderful is just ahead for you in the near future!"

Letter of condolence on the death of a pet

Dear Maura,

I was so sorry to hear of your loss. Pets are more than just animals; they're family members/beloved companions/very special to the people fortunate enough to share their homes and their lives with them. I know how much you loved Spot, and I know you must be grieving now. Please accept my heartfelt condolences.

Sincerely,

Talking with a friend whose relative has been arrested

"I was sorry to hear about *[name]*. *[If you have a good lawyer]* Do you need the name of a good lawyer? I have one.

"Listen, if it's a sore spot, we don't have to talk about it, or if it helps you, we can. But either way, I'm pulling for you . . . and her. I sure hope she gets through this okay. Just let me know if you want to talk . . . or if there's anything concrete I can do to help. Okay?"

Letter covering a check to a stranger whose unfortunate story has touched you

Dear Ms. Williams,

I read the story about you in today's paper/ I saw the story about you on TV. I'd like to help, and I hope others will feel the same. The enclosed check may not be huge, but if enough people respond in a similar way, it might make a difference.

I hope better times are ahead for you, and soon.

Sincerely yours,

Confrontation

Letter confronting someone you suspect of stealing from you

Notes: What you don't want to do is come right out and accuse the person of stealing. First of all, by allowing the person to save face, you make it easier for him to return the stolen item. Second, in these litigious times, if you call someone a thief, you risk a lawsuit—and the fact that you're correct in your accusations may not be a sufficient defense. Last, there is always the chance that you're wrong, that no matter how incriminating the evidence is, the person is in fact not guilty of taking the missing item.

Dear Jim,

How are you? I was so glad you were able to stop over for two days during your trip. It was great to see you! I hope it won't be another three years before I see you again!

Listen, this is a little awkward, but here's why I'm writing. I'm wondering if in your haste to pack, my autographed baseball got mixed in with your things. I know you're no thief, but I think it must have accidentally gotten into your suitcase. I remember seeing it in the guest room before you arrived, and it's not there now. My housecleaner is the only other person who's been in the house since you left, and she says she didn't move it. She certainly didn't take it; she's been working for me for years now. So the only other possibility is that somehow it got mixed in with your things.

Please check to see if you have it, and send it back if you find it. Thanks a lot!

Sincerely,

Confronting someone you suspect of stealing from you

Notes: The important thing is to give the person an "out." If you put her back to the wall and accuse her of stealing, you won't get your item back. You need to offer a plausible alternative: that the item was taken accidentally. That way, she can go home and "find" the item and return it. 🖉

"Hi. How are you, Sherri? Listen, I've got a problem. Do you remember seeing my gold watch when you were here last Friday? I can't find it. I wonder if it might have accidentally fallen into your pocketbook or something. It was careless of me to leave it lying out on the end table.

"Now, nobody else has been around. I've even looked under the furniture. The only thing I can think of is that one of us bumped the table while you were here and accidentally knocked it into your pocketbook.

"Please check the pocketbook you were carrying that night. This has to be the most bizarre accident, but there's no one else who could possibly have it. Thanks!"

Conversation getting rid of an undesirable member of the car pool

"Richard? Hi, I've got kind of an unpleasant matter to discuss with you.

"You know that several of us have talked to you about the way you drive

[or] about the way you're always late when it's your turn to drive

[or] about the way you're so often not ready when we come to get you

[or] about the way you smell of cigarettes— you probably don't realize how rough that is on the rest of us, as nonsmokers.

"Well, every time we talk to you about it, you promise things will change, but they never do. Or if they do, it lasts a week at most. So we've decided that you need to find a different way to get to work.

"I'm sorry, Richard, but a lot of resentment has been building up, so before things get out of hand, we're calling a halt to the arrangement. Take a week if you want to look for another car pool, but after next Monday, you're on your own.

"I hope you understand. And again, I'm sorry. But we're firm about this. No more chances. Okay?"

Coping with a team parent who exhibits bad sportsmanship

"You know, this league is a great learning experience for the kids, isn't it? Learning to play ball . . . learning teamwork . . . and I think learning good sportsmanship is a big part of it too. It's tough—for the kids and for us. We want our team to win. I realize that yelling at the ref is a regular sports tradition. But you know, if we as parents are able to curb our spirit enough to set a great example for the kids, don't you think they'll benefit from that, too?"

Asking someone to stop using a cell phone

"Excuse me, sir, but I am trying to hear the tour guide. I'm sure your call is important, but would you mind stepping off to the side and lowering your voice, so we can hear what the guide has to say? Thank you."

Confronting a guest who is
using derogatory language

"Excuse me, but that sort of talk just isn't allowed in our house, especially in front of our kids. You're entitled to your opinions, but please don't express them here. Now let's talk about something else. Thank you."

Dealing with drop-in guests who
arrive at an inconvenient time

"Oh—gee, Marilyn! It's so good to see you. I'd love to invite you in, but you've caught me at a bad time. Darn it, I wish I had known you were coming so I could have rearranged my schedule! Let's make a plan right now for a time that's good for both of us."

Explaining to a parent why you don't want her child to visit

Notes: No matter how much you want to, you can't just say, "Your brat is always hitting my child and making her cry," or "It's a problem when your child comes over because my child always learns new nasty words from him." Even "Your child steals" is awkward.

There are really only two good dodges. One is to claim that your child is too busy—dance lessons, violin lessons, sports practice, and Scouts, perhaps, if the child is old enough that you can honestly claim such activities. The other, all-purpose excuse better suited for younger kids is the generalized "Our kids really don't play well together. I don't think they're a good combination."

If the other parent insists on a more specific explanation, and you're backed into a corner, give details. If her feelings are hurt after that, it's unfortunate, but she asked. 🖉

"Jennifer is so busy right now with her schoolwork, music lessons, and sports practices that she barely has time for socializing. I guess they'll just have to play together at school."

Reminding a guest that
your home is smoke-free

"John, maybe you didn't realize it, or maybe you just forgot, but this is a smoke-free home. I'm sorry, but I'd appreciate your smoking that outside, please. Thanks."

Telling a guest that he's making a mess

"Oops! Let me guess . . . you've got a new job as a vacuum salesman, and as soon as you drop ashes/crumbs one more time, you're going to whip out your vacuum and show me how well it cleans up spills, right?"

Letter asking your neighbor to clean up his property

Dear Fred,

Letters like these are never easy to write, but I need to discuss the condition of your property.

When we live in the same house day after day and come home to the same yard week after week, we don't *see* them anymore. They're just *there*. You probably don't realize how your house looks. But the paint is peeling, the yard is overgrown and weedy, and the tires and that broken swing set in the front yard do nothing to help the appearance either. If you took a picture of the house and yard from across the street and looked at the photo, you'd probably be amazed . . . and maybe appalled.

Fred, if you ever needed to sell the house or take out a new mortgage, you'd find its appearance working against you. You never know when you might unexpectedly need to do either of those things. Another good reason for keeping the property up is to maintain good relations with your neighbors. Nobody in the world likes it when a neighbor lets his property go. It hurts the appearance and value of all the other properties on the block. Of course, the impression you make on anyone who comes to visit you is another factor.

` *[If the next paragraph isn't applicable, omit it.]*

If you're not feeling well or are overworked and need help, I'd be happy to come over and lend a hand. Or if you need to borrow a lawnmower, call me.

Getting the place put to rights the first time is the hardest, but keeping it up after that should be much easier. And it's worthwhile.

I'm writing this as a friendly neighbor, not an antagonist. I hope you take it in the same spirit.

Your neighbor,

Letter to a neighbor who is trashing your yard

Dear Malcolm,

Hi. I hope this note finds you well. I'm writing to bring your attention to a situation I'm sure you haven't noticed. When your son walks Rex in our yard, he often lets him make a pit stop on our lawn *[or, your son leaves candy wrappers, etc, whatever the problem may be]*. I don't like cleaning it up, and my wife has stepped in it at least once. I thought of talking to your son but decided you might prefer to handle it yourself.

We'd both appreciate it very much if you'd take care of this situation, and we thank you in advance for your help.

Sincerely,

Conversation with a neighbor
who is trashing your yard

"Hi, Malcolm. Got a minute? Listen, I know you don't realize this, or it wouldn't be happening, but when your son walks Rex, a lot of times he lets him make a pit stop on our lawn. It looks bad, it smells bad, and my wife has stepped in it at least once.

"Do you think you could talk to your son and ask him not to let Rex do that. We'd really appreciate it. Thanks a lot, Malcolm!"

Dealing with a guest who has had too much to drink

"I know this may not seem like a very friendly gesture now, but you'll thank me when you're alive in the morning. You've had enough to drink, and you ought to call it a night. You're not fit to drive. *[If he arrived in his own car, without a passenger who could now drive, add]* I'm calling a taxi for you. We can worry about getting your car back to you tomorrow. The important thing now is to get you home safely."

Dealing with someone who is smoking in a public no-smoking area

"Excuse me, sir. I'm sure you didn't realize it or you wouldn't have lit the cigarette, but this *is* a no-smoking area."

Notes: If he says, "Who's going to stop me?" or something of that sort, you can either find a security guard, manager, or whoever's appropriately in charge in that location, or move away. Just don't get into an altercation because these situations can easily escalate into violence.

Asking a friend not to
bring her dog to your house

"I hate to tell you this, but I would rather you didn't bring Tramp with you tomorrow when you come over. I have a couple of friends who are allergic to dogs, and the last time you brought Tramp over, their allergies really kicked up. He's a wonderful animal, and I really enjoy him when I'm at your house, but I think it would be kinder to my other friends if you didn't bring him over to my house again. Please give him a pat or two for me and tell him I'm sorry."

Asking your host to keep his pet in another room when you visit

"Yes, I'd love to come over for dinner Friday night. There's one thing, though, Jack, and if it's going to be a problem, I'll certainly understand.

"I'm terribly afraid of dogs/awfully allergic to cats. Is there any chance you could keep Snowball in another room while I'm there? If not, let's just do our visiting at my house. I don't mind if I'm always the hostess. I really hate to ask you to confine your pet while I'm at your house.

"But if you can do it without it being a problem, I'd love to accept your invitation. Be honest . . . please."

What to say when someone cuts in front of you in line

Notes: The idea is that you want to speak up *loudly* so that the others in line—and perhaps even the cashier or checker—will hear. Then the person will be embarrassed into relinquishing her unfairly taken place.

But if you think there is the slightest possibility that it was an honest error—and I've done it myself—then speak to the cutter quietly at first, only raising your voice if she refuses to back down. ✎

[At first, softly, if you suspect an honest error] "Excuse me—that isn't the end of the line. I've been standing behind this man."

[Next, louder, if the person won't move] "You've cut in. Please go to the end of the line as we all had to do."

Asking a visitor who's too rough
to stop playing with your child

"Jimmy? I realize you don't have kids/Maybe your kids like roughhousing, but that's too much for Evan. He needs a breather. It would be best if you just leave him alone before he really gets upset. Thanks."

Asking a visitor who's too rough to
stop playing with your pet

"Ben? I realize you don't have a dog/I realize your dog is much larger than Tramp, but that's quite a bit rougher than Tramp likes to be played with. Maybe you'd better leave him alone. Not only don't I want him to get hurt, I don't want him to get annoyed and hurt you. And he's getting that look in his eye. So, I'd suggest you just let him be. Thanks."

Letter complaining to your neighbor about a barking dog

Dear Ms. Nelson,

When something in our lives is there all the time, it's easy to get used to it and no longer be aware of it. This may be the case with your dog. I think you don't realize the effect of his frequent barking.

By day, although the constant barking is annoying, it's more bearable. At night, though, it's really bad. The barking wakes us up (and it's all your neighbors, not only our household).

I don't know if the answer lies with disciplining the dog or finding out what he wants and giving it to him, but you must be able to do something. Most dogs aren't that noisy. There has to be a solution.

Several neighbors are reaching the breaking point, but rather than complain to any authorities, I'm hoping I can accomplish something by writing to you and appealing to you, neighbor to neighbor.

Again, I'm writing in a spirit of neighborly cooperation. I hope you will accept this letter in that same spirit . . . and will do something to alleviate the situation. Thank you.

Sincerely yours,

Talking to your neighbor about tree limbs that extend over your property

"Hi, Sally. May I talk to you for a second? Listen, what can we do about that tree that hangs over the fence? You know, as pretty as it is, it drops leaves and blossoms on my side of the fence all the time. And I'd love not to have that cleanup problem.

"Would you be willing to cut off the limbs that extend over my property? Or I could do it or have it done. Which option works for you?"

Asking friends not to phone before or after a certain hour

"Do you mind calling before 8:30 from now on? I know 8:45 isn't that late in the evening, but we wind down early/we go to bed early/in our house the evening is family time. So, we really try to discourage people from calling after 8:30. Thanks, I appreciate it."

[Or]

"Do you mind calling after 9:00 A.M.? I am not an early bird. I don't get up till 7:30, and sometimes I sleep later. Then I have my morning routine, and I like to get through it without being sidetracked. Besides, I wake up slowly, and I prefer not to talk to people till I'm really functioning, which is usually after 9:00. Thanks, I appreciate it."

Letter asking a friend not to phone so often

Dear Maureen,

Sometimes life is about choices. You want to go to two different restaurants, but you're just eating out one night this week. Or, you want to go to your son's soccer game and your daughter's Girl Scout presentation, but they're both at the same time . . . Well, you get the idea.

My problem is that I love to talk to my friends on the phone, but there are so many other things I need to get done. The more I talk to friends, the less time I have for all that other stuff. So I'm asking my friends who call frequently to please call less often.

And that includes you.

Please don't misunderstand—I love talking to you. But I can't talk to you as often as I do and still get everything done. I want to spend more time with the kids, keep the house a little neater, and . . . Well, you know all the things there are to do.

Please don't take this note the wrong way. I'm no less eager to talk to you than before. But I have to prioritize. As I said, life is about choices.

Thanks for understanding.

Your friend,

Chastising a dinner guest
who regularly shows up late

"Tom? May I ask you a favor? I need for you to show up on time when I invite you for dinner. I don't know if you think you're doing me a favor by giving me extra time to get ready, but it really doesn't work out.

"When I ask you to show up at 5:30, that's what I *mean.* And if I've planned to serve drinks at 5:30 and dinner at six, it's a problem when you don't show up until 6:15.

"It's even worse if dinner happens to finish cooking a little ahead of schedule, and I'm ready to serve at 5:45 . . . but you're not there yet.

"So, please, remember that when I say, 'Come for drinks at 5:30,' I mean it. Thanks."

Asking for, or demanding, the return of a borrowed item

"I hate to have to ask *[again]*, but you know that sweater I lent you two weeks ago/last month/to wear last Saturday? I'm sure you've just forgotten *[again]*, but I'd really like it back. Can you bring it over later?/Can you bring it to work tomorrow and give it me then?/Will you please drop it in the mail to me today? Thanks."

Love/Romance

Writing a classified personal ad

Notes: Anybody can write an ordinary ad that just gives the facts, but that's not the way to get maximum attention. Still, there are times when that may be what you want to do—for example, in a publication where line space is terribly expensive, or if you're on a very tight budget. So what *are* those confusing abbreviations you see in those ads?

DWPF [divorced white Protestant female], 36, 1 child, ISO [in search of] S/D/W WCM [single/divorced/widowed white Christian male], profl [professional], 34–45, Kennewick area. Love golf, movies, bridge, jogging, dining out or eating in (good cook). Box 861.

But if you can afford the space, try to be clever. Even if the whole ad isn't catchy, at least try for an attention-grabbing opening line (see the example on the next page).

Win a classy divorcee of 42, kids grown, trim figure! Just send 25 box tops and an essay of 50 words or more . . .

No, I'm not perfect! And I don't expect you to be, either . . .

This ad guaranteed 100% BS-free! . . . ✍

Replying to a classified personal ad

Notes: Again, as with placing an ad, the trick is to sound appealing—and a little out of the ordinary. The person who placed the ad may have gotten an avalanche of replies. He probably won't go out with all the women who responded; he may not even reply to every one. You want to be sure that yours is one of the ones that is acted on.

Will he like you once you're out together? Help with that problem would be the subject of an entirely different book! First, you have to get to Point A—the point at which your letter, in response to the ad, attracts the reader's attention and is acted on.

How to do it? Sound appealing . . . and clever or different or funny. Then describe yourself in terms that are honest but that will still reel in your fish. If you're deceptive or downright deceitful, he will be disappointed—*and* discouraged about your honesty—when he finally meets you. But if you're brutally honest ("I'm 100 pounds overweight," "I have more wrinkles than unironed cotton"), you'll scare him off.

What to do? Play up your good points, and don't mention your less-than-appealing aspects.

You don't have to say you're fat as long as you don't claim to be "slim" or "trim" or to have a "good figure." If you lack sparkle, don't claim "great personality"; there are other things you can say about yourself that are true: "easygoing," "understanding," "caring," "compassionate," or "romantic" perhaps? 🖊

Dear Charming Lady/Dear Intriguing-Sounding Gent/Dear Clever Ad-Writer,

The greatest journeys of life begin with a single step. You took a step when you wrote the ad that caught my eye. I'm taking a step by writing back. Perhaps we will find ourselves journeying together . . . but we'll never know till we take that next step. How about dinner together, to get to know each other better?

Let me tell you a little about me: I'm . . . .

[Or]

Hello!

If you're even half as clever/funny/intriguing as your ad, dinner with you will be an experience to be remembered. Would you like to give me a chance to find out?

My name is _____. I'm . . .

Rejecting a respondent to your personal ad

Dear George,

Thank you for replying to my ad. I have received several intriguing responses, and right now I don't have the time to go out with all of the other men who replied. But I do thank you for your answer and wish you much good luck. I hope you find the right person soon!

Sincerely,

"Box 897"

Ending a dating relationship by letter

Dear Eric,

Some things are never easy to say. "It's over" is one of them. Unfortunately, that's the message I need to convey with this letter. I think you know my reasons.

[Or] I'm not getting what I want out of the relationship, and the longer I procrastinate, the harder it will be, so let me end this while it's still relatively easy to do.

[Or] Your behavior/The unfortunate scene/Our disagreement the other night demonstrated that we aren't suited for each other.

[Or] You know that the one thing I will not put up with is dishonesty/violence/drunkenness/_____.

Thank you for the good times, and we did have some good times, but I need to call an end to it. Please don't call me again. I am not going to change my mind.

I wish you the best of luck in the future.

Sincerely,

Returning a gift from an admirer by mail

Dear Marco,

The pendant is exquisite—and it was very sweet of you to give it to me—but I'm returning it with this note. It simply isn't appropriate. This necklace is the sort of gift a boyfriend might give his girlfriend, and you're *not* my boyfriend. I don't see our relationship in that light in the future either, so I must return the gift.

Thank you again for your thoughtful generosity. You certainly have good taste.

Sincerely,

Refusing a gift from an admirer

"Jack, this gift is very generous—and it's absolutely gorgeous—but I have to give it back to you. A ring really isn't appropriate. I can't accept this kind of a gift from a friend.

"Jack, I don't consider you my boyfriend, and I'm not looking to get into that sort of relationship with you so you can see why I wouldn't feel right about accepting this gift. Please don't protest. It was extremely generous of you—and you have great taste—but I need to give it back to you."

Announcing a broken engagement

Dear Vanessa,

Sometimes things don't work out the way we expect them to. Evan and I are no longer planning to get married. I'm not going to go into all the details, but I hope that, in the long run, it will prove to be for the best. I just wanted to let you and my other out-of-town friends and relatives know.

My best to you and the rest of the "Cincinnati crowd."

Love,

Telling people that you are getting divorced

"I don't want to make a dramatic announcement out of this, but I ought to tell you that Pat and I are ending our marriage. I'll be moving/I've moved out/I'll be keeping the house. I'll give you my new phone number/I'm getting an unlisted number, and for now I'm not giving it to anyone but my mom/I'm keeping the same phone number.

[To be added with a smile, if you want to cut off inquiries of "What happened?"] "This isn't a press conference, so I won't be taking questions."

Discouraging a persistent suitor

"I may admire someone who doesn't let life discourage him easily, but that still doesn't affect my answer. The answer is no. And if you ask me five more times, the answer is still going to be no. *[In particularly severe cases, add]* Please stop beating your head against a brick wall and give it up."

Declining a blind date

"I've had enough bad experiences with blind dates that I have a policy against accepting them. Even if your friend is on the list of One Hundred Most Eligible Bachelors/Single Women, I'm going to say no. It's nothing against you or your friend . . . who's probably a charming/lovely person. I just don't accept blind dates, okay? Thanks."

Taking a Stand

Refusing to lend personal property

"Look, accidents happen. And the accident that happens to my car while you're driving it/to my lawnmower while you're using it/ to my clothes while you're wearing them might not be your fault. It might be the fault of the idiot behind you, or the one next to you./It might be a rock in your yard that happens to damage my mower./It might be the jerk next to you who spills wine on my sweater while you're wearing it. But it will still involve my car/mower/sweater. And it will still happen while it's in your possession.

"Now, I value our friendship. And that friendship is going to be strained if something happens to my car/mower/sweater while you've got it.

"So, for the sake of our friendship, not to mention my peace of mind, I'm going to have to say no."

Refusing to let a friend
drive your brand-new car

"I sure don't blame you for wanting to try out my car! But what if anything happened to it? Even driving twenty miles per hour on deserted streets, something *could* happen. And you'd feel awful . . . maybe even worse than I'd feel.

"So I'm doing us both a favor and saying no."

Letter declining a semiformal invitation

Dear Myrna and Clay,

Thank you so much for your kind invitation. Unfortunately, Eric and I must decline with thanks. We are already committed for that date. Our best wishes to you on this happy occasion and always.

Sincerely,

Returning an inappropriate gift by mail

Dear Misty,

Thank you so much for the generous gift . . . but, as beautiful as it is, I simply can't accept your late mother's necklace. I don't feel it's appropriate for me to wear it. I didn't even know your mother. This is an heirloom. A family member should be wearing it—if not you then your sister, perhaps, or another female relative—and so I'm returning it to you with thanks, and with regret.

Sincerely,

Refusing an inappropriate gift

"Thanks, Dennis, but I can't accept the baseball glove with DiMaggio's autograph . . . that was your dad's! This glove belongs in the family! It's a treasure, a family keepsake, and it wouldn't be right for me to take it. I appreciate the thought, but please keep the glove."

Declining an invitation from someone you don't want to socialize with

"I'm sorry . . . I can't. My schedule's so crowded these days my children have to make appointments to see me!" *[Or, if you don't have kids but do own a dog]* " . . . my dog has to make appointments with me to get walked." *[Or]* "I'm sorry. I'm spread way too thin right now. I know you can appreciate the feeling. Thanks anyway for the invitation."

Declining to buy cookies from a coworker for her child's fundraiser

"I'm sorry, but I already have so many cookies at home from people who sold them to my husband that I could open a cookie store." *[Or]* "I'm on a diet. You don't want to do that to me, do you? Do your bit for another worthy cause—my waistline—and keep those cookies away from me."

[Or] "My husband/wife is on a diet/diabetic, and I don't want to bring cookies into the house. It wouldn't be fair, especially since I just don't eat that many sweets. I'm sure you understand."

Declining to buy cookies
from a neighborhood child

"I'm sorry, but I just wouldn't eat them. I don't care for cookies."

[Or] "I'm on a diet." *[Or]* "I'm not allowed to eat sweets. Doctor's orders.

"I know your group is a worthwhile organization, but it's kind of silly for me to buy cookies if I'm not going to eat them. Come back another time when you're selling something different. Okay?"

[Optional: "I'd be glad to give you a small donation, though. Here's $____ for your group."]

Declining an invitation to
a high-stakes poker game

"Sorry, I only enjoy low-stakes games. I like to play for fun, and it isn't fun when I have to worry about how much I'm betting. I like penny-ante, nickel-and-dime games *[or whatever your comfort level is],* where everyone's in it for the fun, not the money, and there's no risk of someone losing too much."

What to say when you need to decline your neighbor who is collecting for a charity

"Gee, I hate to say no to a neighbor, Emily. But the reality is, I have certain charities I give to at certain times. Every year I work out a budget for my donations, and I really try to stick to it. Unfortunately, this group isn't on my list. Perhaps if I learned more about it, I could include it for next year. Do you have any literature?

"The world needs more people who'll help charitable causes like you're doing. You're a good person. Thanks for dropping in, and I hope you get better results from the rest of the neighbors.

[If she says, "Everyone else on the block is giving"] "Well, that's great. Then my choice to give elsewhere doesn't hurt, because you're already collecting plenty of money."

[If she says, "It's a good charity. What have you got against it?"] "I didn't say I have anything against your group. I said I budget my charity donations, certain causes at certain times, and this one isn't on the list. If you'd like to leave me some literature to read, I'll be happy to look at it and think about whether I want to include it next year."

What to say when your friend asks your opinion of her purchase—and you hate it

Notes: The trick here, as with thank-you notes for gifts that are inappropriate (see page 7) is to find something you *can* compliment honestly. Is the suit the latest cut even though it makes the man look fat, or stuffy, or pretentious? Compliment its trendiness. Is the house in a dubious neighborhood but plenty spacious? Comment on its roominess. If it's old and dark, can you compliment it on its antique charm? If it's cramped, does it have a yard worth ooohing and aaaahhing over?

[Is the car ugly but a proven mileage winner?] "I hear you get great mileage with those! Smart choice!"

[Is the dress a hideous print but a bright color?] "That's the cheeriest dress I've seen in a long time!"

Answering questions about your illness without eliciting sympathy

"Thank you for asking. The chemo is rough but necessary, and I hope it's helping. Sometimes I think the way people feel sorry for me is rougher than the illness itself. People either are afraid to ask at all or fall all over me with sympathy. I have no problem answering questions, but I don't like all the pity. I have every intention of getting through this!"

Declining to discuss your serious illness

"Thank you for asking. I'm doing as well as can be expected. You know I've been ill, but it does no good to dwell on it; I'd much rather talk about something else."

Declining to give advice

"I don't like to tell people what to do. If you take my advice, and things don't work out the way you want, you're going to remember that I told you what to do. And, face it, I'm not a psychologist, or a human relations expert, or Dear Abby. So, what qualifies me to tell you how to run your life?"

Explaining to your host why you haven't eaten much of a food you hate

"To be perfectly honest, lima beans aren't one of my favorite foods, but I do find these tastier than usual. It's a tribute to your cooking that I ate as much as I did."

Refusing to take sides in a disagreement

"I'm not getting into the middle of this quarrel. You're both my friends, and I can't possibly take sides or even arbitrate. You'll have to work it out. Call me 'Switzerland'—I'm remaining neutral."

Deflecting unwanted advice

"Thanks for the advice, but I think I need to sort my own way through this. And if things don't work out right, this way I have no one but myself to blame. I appreciate your trying to help, though. Really."

Answering your teenager's questions
about your past behavior

"Obviously I did some things I shouldn't have; I was a teenager. But I'm *not* going into specifics with you. In looking back, I'm not pleased or proud of what I did, and I'd like to think you wouldn't make the same mistakes I did. Of course, I'd like to think you wouldn't make *any* mistakes. I'd like to think you wouldn't drive too fast or without seat belts, mess with drugs, drink too much, have premarital sex—and certainly the times have changed on *that* one—in my day, AIDS wasn't the issue it is now. *[Fill in whatever else is appropriate for you to mention to your child]*."

Avoiding volatile discussions

"There are certain topics I don't like to talk about. That list includes most topics that can lead to strong differences of opinion. Call me a pacifist, but I don't enjoy anything that resembles fighting or conversations that cause tension. It's just not my idea of a good time.

"Some people believe that politics and religion are too controversial to talk about in public. Now, I don't know if religion is still such a hot-button topic, but discussing politics—in the larger sense of the word—has certainly led to fights and caused hard feelings. So, if you don't mind, leave me out of this one."

What to say when you can't remember a person's name

"Hi! I haven't seen you since the last PTA meeting. How've you been? And the family? What's new?" *[And, if you feel honesty is called for, add]* "You know, I have to be honest—this is terrible, but I am drawing a complete blank on your name! I know exactly who you are, but . . ."

What to say when you don't recognize someone who knows you

"You know, I could pretend to remember your name while desperately groping through my memory, but I'm going to play it straight and confess. Could you help me out here? Obviously I'd never make it in politics! I'm sorry, but what's your name again?"

Answering "And what do *you* do?"

Note: It's a little difficult to get out of answering this one, but if you're absolutely set on it, a joke is the best way to deflect the question.

- "Oh, I'm a bookie."
- "I'm a Russian spy. Business is slow these days. Do you need any spying done? I'm offering a cut-rate special!"
- "Well, I *was* the human cannonball with the circus . . . but I was fired from my job."

Refusing to lie to a friend's spouse

"I'm a miserable liar, and I don't think I could get away with it, so I wouldn't be of any help to you. *[Add, if you want]* Even if I did, I'd be too concerned he'd find out later on and tell *my* husband, and then I'd be in the doghouse!

Deflecting a too-personal question

"That's very funny! Do you know, someone *actually asked me that* recently! They weren't kidding like you . . . they really expected me to answer!"
[Or]
"Gee . . . are you writing a book about me?"

Refusing to answer a question

"That's classified information. I could tell you . . . but then I'd have to kill you."

Apologies/Excuses/
Mending Fences

Letter accepting overtures
of renewed friendship

Dear Dana,

Thank you! One of us had to be big enough to break the ice, which is an appropriate metaphor, given the recent chill between us. I'm glad you did. Of course I want to be friends again!

Let's meet after work one day next week and have dinner together. I'm free Monday, Tuesday, and Thursday. Would one of those evenings work for you? Call me—same home number as always, or my new work number is 555-9654—and let me know which night is best for you.

And again—thanks!

Sincerely,

Letter apologizing for an old insult

Dear Barb,

Having reached the half-century mark/Having started a New Year/Having recently grown more introspective, I've been doing some thinking.

As a result, I'm writing this note to apologize for that incident last February/ten years ago/at Emily's wedding. I know from your attitude toward me ever since that I hurt you/Although you've treated me just the same since then, I know I was wrong and must have hurt your feelings.

I can't take back what I said/did, but I *can* apologize. It may be a bit late, but I'm hoping you'll agree with the old adage, "Better late than never." Please accept this sincere, if belated, apology.

Sincerely,

Letter accepting an apology

Dear Rob,

Thank you for apologizing for what you said about me/what you did at the Christmas party/breaking a confidence/*[other]*. I appreciate the apology, and of course I accept. Now let's put the whole mess behind us. How about lunch next week? Call me and let me know what day is good for you.

Sincerely,

Letter admitting to and apologizing for causing damage at a friend's house

Dear Tom,

I'm not sure if this is a letter or a confession. I'm guilty, I'm embarrassed, and the longer I keep quiet about it, the more guilty and the more embarrassed I'll be. So here's what I need to tell you:

Last weekend, when I was at your house, I accidentally knocked over your delicate clock. When I picked it up, it had stopped running. You were out of the room at the time. So I put it back on the table and said nothing to you.

[Or] Last weekend, when I was a guest at your house, you told me to help myself to anything I wanted. When I helped myself to some vodka from your liquor cabinet, I broke the bottle. I cleaned up the mess, but I didn't say anything.

[Or whatever the situation might be.]

The longer I put off telling you, the more embarrassed I become. I'm not cut out for a life of crime. It's time to come clean, apologize, and pay for the damages. Please let me know how much I owe you.

I regret my cowardice even more than my clumsiness. Please forgive me.

Sincerely,

Letter apologizing for accidentally taking something belonging to your host

Dear Annamarie,

Is my face red! When I got home from my weekend at your house and unpacked my suitcase, I found your bedside clock inside. I can just see how it happened: I took my clothes out of the closet, laid them on the night table before packing them, and when I picked them up, I scooped up the clock as well. That's some way to pay you back for your hospitality . . . walking off with your clock!

I'm enclosing the clock as well as a small token of my appreciation for a delightful weekend (and my profound regret at this unfortunate incident). Thanks again for a wonderful time!

Sincerely,

Letter of apology for arriving at a social occasion with a contagious ailment

Dear Jeannie,

I'm sorry! I think I made a poor decision. In my desire not to mess you up by canceling at the last minute—and because I didn't want to miss out on one of your wonderful dinner parties/great parties/fun evenings—I tried to tell myself, "It's just a little sniffle," when the more considerate thing might have been to stay home and keep my germs at home with me.

I hope nobody caught it from me.

I had a wonderful time! I just hope that in enjoying the fun I didn't also spread germs. Forgive me?

Thanks,

Conversation with your child's friend's parent when you discover your child has head lice right after a sleepover

"Hi, Karen? It's me, Jeannie. Listen, this is kind of embarrassing, but here goes . . . I think you'd better check Steffi's head . . . and wash her sheets in very hot water. I just found out Kayla has head lice, and I'm upset to think she could have given them to Steffi when she slept at your house the night before last.

"I'm really red-faced over this, but I thought I'd better call you as soon as I found out.

"Thanks for not making a fuss about it."

Letter apologizing for misbehavior or poor judgment

Dear Melanie,

Is my face red! It's the color it should have been Saturday night when I told that joke that was in such poor taste/when I drank too much and probably made a damn fool of myself.

I hope I didn't offend you *[add if appropriate]* and your other guests. If I promise not to do it again, will you forgive me?

I am truly embarrassed and v*ery* sorry. Please accept my most profound apologies.

Sincerely,

Letter apologizing for a social gaffe

Dear Mona,

Do I feel like an idiot! Breaking that pretty flowerpot was bad enough, but getting the dirt all over your carpet was even worse. While I win Klutz of the Year award, you win an award for compassion and composure under duress. You handled my clumsy blunder with such finesse.

I feel totally distraught over the damage I did. I should, at the very least, have been the one to drag out the vacuum and get that dirt out of your immaculate carpet! Please accept my abject and sincere apologies once again.

Your red-faced friend,

Conciliatory letter

Dear Ed,

It's been awhile. And it's a shame. Friends should be able to get past "incidents" or disagreements and go on enjoying each other's companionship.

Do you think we can put the past behind us? Let's have lunch next week and pick up where we left off. Are you agreeable? Call me. My number hasn't changed.

Hoping to hear from you—

Delicate Situations

Answering your child's questions about Santa

"You want the truth? There is a Santa . . . but he's not a jolly man in a red suit who puts presents under the tree. Your dad and I do that. Santa is the Christmas spirit. You know how everyone's nicer to everyone else around Christmastime? Naturally, kids are being good so they'll get lots of presents. But grownups are nicer to each other too. Have you noticed the way people say hello to strangers? The way they hold doors open for each other and smile? The way people are nicer than usual? Well, that's the Christmas spirit—and that's what Santa Claus really is. Santa Claus is the Christmas spirit.

"Wouldn't it be nice if people behaved like that all year long?"

What to say to a mother whose baby or child is *not* cute

Note: If the infant is adorable, say so, or call her "precious," and that's all you have to say. The problem arises when the baby is not going to win any beauty contests. ✐

"Goodness, what bright eyes! I can tell she's going to graduate at the head of her class."

"He's got his dad's mouth. Your husband must be really proud."

"She has so much hair for a child that age. Good grief, I'm impressed."

"Plenty of meat on his bones. He'll grow up big and strong for sure!"

"She's nice and trim. I'm jealous . . . she'll never have a weight problem."

"Oh—look at that smile. How wonderful to see such a happy child!"

"He's certainly active. Isn't that supposed to be a sign of intelligence?"

What to say to the mother who has just had a child who is physically or mentally challenged

"Congratulations! He certainly is a cute/big/curly-haired baby. I know you're going to be a wonderful mother—he's a lucky kid to have you for a mom. I know you have a challenge ahead, but I also know you're up to it."

"I hope you have lots of pleasure with him."

Notes: Do not offer sympathy. You still say, "Congratulations." And if the child is cute or has a precious face or lots of curly hair or anything else you can comment on positively, you do. ✎

Invitations/Announcements

Informal letter inviting people to your house

Dear Bert and Linda,

We're having a few people over for dinner on Saturday the 11th, and we would very much like you to be part of the group. It's an informal gathering; no special occasion, so dress casually. Please tell me you'll be part of it. Plan on being here at 5:00 for drinks. Hope you can make it!

Always,

Writing to explain to someone why you no longer will be inviting him/her to your house

Dear Gerri,

This isn't an easy letter to write. Here's the problem: The other night, at our house, you once again made remarks about people of a certain ethnic group. Two of the others who were there have friends or relatives within that group. And they were offended. *[Or:]* Saturday night, at dinner at my house, you once again overindulged in alcohol, and once again offended people with your behavior. You're entitled to do whatever you want in your own home, but when you offend my guests, then as the hostess, it becomes my problem. We've talked about this before, but despite your promises, nothing seems to have changed. *[Or whatever the problem is. Those are the two most common.]*

Though I still think of you as my friend, I'm afraid we'll have to confine our visits to different circumstances. We could have lunches together downtown, or one-on-one visits at my house or yours on a weekend afternoon.

This hasn't been an easy letter to write, and I hope it doesn't damage our relationship.

As always,

Letter declining an invitation from a former in-law, when you fear family repercussions for keeping up a relationship

Dear Marilyn,

This is one of the most difficult letters I've ever had to write. You know how fond I've always been of you, and what happened between you and Jack is your business. But here's the situation:

I'm under a great deal of pressure from the family because of my having continued to socialize with you. I could stand up for my principles and continue seeing you socially, starting with accepting your invitation to the Labor Day picnic at your house. But I'd be in one huge mess with the family if I did. It's a heck of a predicament.

I'm hearing about it from all sides, and it's clear that I'm creating a rift by remaining in social contact with you. And so, for the sake of peace in the family, I must decline your invitation . . . and any future invitation. Please understand. Above all, please accept that this in no way reflects a change of feelings about you. I still think you're a wonderful person.

May life bring you everything you want and then some. My sincere best wishes to you.

With regret,

Adoption announcement

We are pleased to announce a new addition to our family. We have adopted Sean, age three months, a charming, smiling, delightful baby. We wish you as much happiness as Sean is giving us.

PART TWO
Personal Business

Resignation/Dismissal

Resigning from a job

"Mrs. Brown, may I talk to you for a minute? It's been a pleasure taking care of your lawn all this time, but I'm not going to be mowing lawns anymore. You know I'm going away to college./I have a health problem./I can't get into the reason, but it's personal and has nothing to do with you.

"I'll continue doing your lawn for the next two weeks/month to give you a chance to find someone else. *[If applicable, add]* I have a friend/I know a company named *[name]* I'd be glad to recommend. I'm sure they would do a fine job. I can give you their number, if you'd like.

"Best of luck to you in the future, Mrs. Brown. Thank you for being a good customer."

Terminating someone's employment (in person)

"Jennie? May I talk to you for a minute? I'm sorry to tell you that I won't need your help as a babysitter/housecleaner any longer.

[Or] Because of what happened last week, I felt it would be best to look for another babysitter/housecleaner, and I've found someone.

[Or] For personal reasons, I felt it was best if I found another babysitter/housecleaner; this is no reflection on the quality of your work. The end of this week will be the last time I'll need your help.

[If applicable, insert next paragraph.]

"I would be happy to give you a good reference, if you wanted to give my name to anyone who's thinking of hiring you.

[If applicable, insert next paragraph.]

"I'm giving you a little something extra in your pay.

"Thank you for all your help."

Recommendations

Employment recommendation
for a personal acquaintance

To Whom It May Concern:

I am pleased to recommend John for your consideration. I have known John for ten years and have found him to be *[use any of the following qualities, if true and if relevant to the position in question, without using so many that you overdo it, or add others you may think of that are particularly appropriate]* diligent, hard working, honest, detail-oriented, dedicated, honorable, a person who takes initiative, adaptable, creative, imaginative, a good leader, a great team worker, persuasive, a person of great ingenuity, dedicated, a great problem-solver. I believe he would be a great addition to your organization.

If you have any questions or would like further information, please don't hesitate to write to me at the address given above or call me at 555-2490.

Sincerely yours,

Nonemployment recommendation
for a personal acquaintance

To Whom It May Concern:

It is my pleasure to recommend Sara to you for admission to *[name of college, club, or other]*. I think she will be a valuable addition to your roster of members *[or]* students. In the five years I have known her, I have found her to be *[list a few qualities that are true of the person and applicable to the situation; for a club, you might say]* sociable, a good leader, a person of great tact, amiable, easy to get along with, witty, entertaining, reliable, responsible; *[for college admission, you might say]* respectful, studious, dedicated, hard working, responsible, goal-oriented, a person who takes initiative, mature, a good leader, sensible.

If you have any further questions, please do not hesitate to contact me at the address given above or call me at 555-3679.

Sincerely yours,

Letter of reference for a household service provider

To Whom It May Concern:

Susan has worked for us as a babysitter/house-cleaner for ___ years, and we have found her to be *[choose any of the following that apply to the person and to the position in question; add any other relevant qualities that you may think of]* reliable, prompt, honest, diligent, hard working, thorough, good with kids, and easy to get along with.

[Add one of the following, if applicable and if you want to] Susan still cleans/baby-sits for us part-time. She no longer baby-sits for us only because our child no longer needs a sitter. Susan no longer cleans for us only because we are now cleaning the house ourselves/because we decided on a full-time cleaning person and she is not available full-time/because we no longer need a full-time cleaning person and have hired a part-timer.

I have no hesitation in recommending Susan to you. I will be glad to answer any further questions —you may call me at 555-2762 or write to the address above.

Sincerely yours,

Soliciting/Fundraising/ Fee Adjusting

Verbal request for payment of an overdue personal loan

"Ken, you know, it's been ____ weeks/months since I lent you that $____. Our understanding at the time was that you'd be paying me back in ____ days/weeks/months. But so far you haven't returned the money/you've returned only $____ of it. It's time I got my money back. I'd like to have payment by the end of this week/within a week/in a day or two. I'm sure I can count on you to do the honorable thing. I'll expect payment in full on *[date or day]*. Thank you."

Letter explaining your rate increase for household services

Dear Mr. Smith:

No one likes to see prices go up, but eventually all service providers have to raise their prices—the supermarket, the gas station, clothing stores, and me. As the cost of living goes up, prices go up all over. *[If applicable, such as for yard work, add]* My costs of doing business—for example, gasoline for the lawnmower, the cost of repair and maintenance, and the cost of other tools I need for my work—have risen as well. Unfortunately I need to pass these costs along in order for my business to remain profitable.

Effective on *[date]*, my rates will be _____. Thank you for understanding.

Sincerely yours,

Letter requesting a reference

Dear Mary,

As you may know, I have been searching for a better employment situation, and I think I've found what I am looking for. The company in question is asking for three letters of reference. Since we are business friends, you are in a position of being able to talk about me in both a business and a personal context.

You know what my business capabilities are as well as what kind of person I am. I wonder if I could ask you to write a letter that would talk about me in both contexts. The letter would go to *[name, position, company, address].* If you are willing to provide the letter, you can mail it directly to the company, and then just call to let me know.

I really appreciate the favor. If, however, you're uncomfortable with this request for any reason, please let me know.

Sincerely yours,

Letter requesting a credit reference

Dear Ms. Cosgrove:

I have recently applied for a credit account with the XYZ Company, and they've requested references from other local merchants I do business with. Since I've had an account with your firm for quite a few years now, I wonder if you would mind writing a brief note to Jim Henderson at XYZ, telling him what my credit record has been with you.

I appreciate your help in this matter and thank you in advance.

Sincerely yours,

Letter soliciting household work

Dear Mr. Jones,

My name is _____, and I have been doing yard work/babysitting in the area for _____ months/years. I am reliable, conscientious, hard working, reasonably priced, and can provide references on request. *[Add either of the following if applicable]* I have all the necessary equipment to take care of your yard, whether you simply want your lawn mowed or want weeding, pruning, and other work in addition.

[Or] I am very good with kids. I get them involved in a variety of games, crafts projects, and activities, according to their ages.

Some of the other people I have done work for locally include the Smiths and the Browns. *[If you are still in school or a local college]* I am _____ years old and go to _____.

If you would like to hire me to do yard work/babysitting for you or simply want to talk to me and perhaps ask me for further information, you can reach me at 555-3233. Thank you for considering me.

Sincerely yours,

Complaints/Rejections

Letter of complaint about a defective or unsatisfactory product

To Whom It May Concern:

On *[date]* I purchased *[name or describe product]* from you/from *[name of store or other sales outlet]*. Unfortunately, I find myself disappointed in the quality of this product because *[describe the defect or the reason the product is not satisfactory]*. I am sure you stand behind the merchandise you sell/manufacture, and so I am requesting a refund/replacement/repair.

How would you like me to return the *[product]*?/What mailing address should I use? Thank you in advance for your help.

Sincerely yours,

Requesting the correction of a bill

"Good morning/afternoon. This is *[your name, your account number or other identifying information]*. I've received a bill from you dated ____ for $____, and I believe a mistake has been made.

"I believe the charge for $____ should not be there because ____ *[or]* I believe the charge for $____ is a wrong amount because ____. I would like authorization to adjust the amount/remove that charge before paying my bill for what I believe is the correct amount. Can you handle that for me? Thank you."

Letter requesting the correction of a bill

To Whom It May Concern:

This is in reference to account number ____ *[or other identifying information]*. I've received a bill from you dated _____ for $____, and I believe a mistake has been made.

I believe the charge for $_____ should not be there because _____ *[or]* I believe the charge for $_____ is a wrong amount because _____. I am enclosing a check paying what I believe is the correct amount. I would appreciate an adjusted bill correcting the error. Thank you in advance for your attention to this matter.

Sincerely yours,

Refusing to cosign a loan

"I'm sorry, but I don't think that I can help you. My credit is pretty well up to its limit now."

[Or] "I need to save whatever credit I have left because I'm planning to make a major purchase soon myself. If I cosign your loan, my own application will be declined. Unfortunately I'm just not in a position to be able to help you without hurting myself."

Letter declining a job offer

Dear Ms. Voorhees:

Thank you for letting me know that Amalgamated would like me to take the available position as collections supervisor. I regret to tell you that I have accepted a position elsewhere in the meanwhile/that I have decided against accepting the position.

My thanks for your interest, and my best wishes to you.

Sincerely yours,

Letter declining a volunteer position

Dear Ms. Richards:

This is with reference to your asking me to chair the school's carnival committee. Although I admire the work done by the Meadowbrook PTA and the importance of the carnival as our annual fundraiser, I have too many conflicting commitments to chair the carnival this year. I'm afraid both the quality of my work as carnival chair and my other obligations would suffer if I spread myself too thin. Therefore I must decline.

Of course our family will attend the carnival, and I intend to remain an active member of the PTA.

Sincerely yours,

Letter declining a request for a loan

Dear Paul,

I hate to say no to a friend, but I have to decline your request for a loan.

[Include either or both of the following paragraphs]

I have had bad experiences in the past with lending money to friends and relatives. And the problem is not just getting my money back but the bad feelings that resulted, both on my part when I wasn't repaid promptly and on their parts when I finally had to ask them to please repay me. I value our relationship too much to risk jeopardizing it, and I have made a promise to myself that I would not lend money again.

I have my own financial needs and situations, and I am just not in a position to make a loan at this point.

I hope you understand.

Sincerely,

Letter complaining to a
restaurant about poor food

To Whom It May Concern:

On *[date]* I visited your restaurant, looking forward to a good meal *[add, if applicable]* such as I have had there in the past. Unfortunately, I was vastly disappointed in the *[name(s) of food(s) that disappointed you]* because *[give one or more concrete reasons, such as]* the sauce was too bland/the food was lukewarm at best/the vegetables were mushy/the sauce was terribly greasy/the meat was exceedingly tough/the portions were tiny.

I am very disappointed in *[name of restaurant]*. I had expected better. I will not be returning, and I wanted you to know why so perhaps you can better serve future customers.

Sincerely yours,

Letter complaining to a restaurant about unsanitary conditions

To Whom It May Concern:

On *[date]* I visited your restaurant and was appalled at *[whichever of the following applies:]* finding hair in the *[name of food]*/finding an insect in the *[name of food]*/the gross condition of the restroom/the greasy/dirty utensils/the overall lack of cleanliness in the restaurant/the filthiness of the floor.

I had expected better of *[name of restaurant]*. I will not be returning, and I wanted you to know why so perhaps you can better serve future customers.

Sincerely yours,

Advertisements

Advertisement for an apartment or house for rent

Notes: The format of a for-rent ad varies from area to area. More or fewer words may be abbreviated, according to local custom and according to the per-line rate of your local newspaper's classified ads section. You would be best off to check comparable ads in your local paper (or, if the ad is for a *Pennysaver* or other specialty paper, check in that publication) to see what the local custom is and whether the ads typically begin with the number of rooms or with the area or street where the house/apartment is located.

Be sure to include the number of rooms, number of bathrooms, location, rental price, and your phone number. Beyond that, since you want to make the house/apartment sound as attractive as possible, include any special features or advantages, such as a two-car garage, a wood-burning fireplace, new carpets/tile floors/parquet floors, all appliances included, wooded lot, terrace, swimming pool, huge living room, secluded, good schools, two blocks from the police station, walk to the bus stop/train station, convenient to shopping, or a garage apartment—great privacy.

You probably ought to add "No broker's fee," so readers know that you are the owner and they don't need to pay a rental broker's commission. You also should state when the house/apartment is available. ✒

Here's a sample ad, with typical abbreviations (remember, though, that these vary from area to area):

Kensington area, 3 bdrms/2 bath gdn apt, first flr, new appls incl washer/dryer, secure/safe, good nbrhd, 1 blk bus stop, nr all shopng, 2 assigned parkg places, playgrnd, only $900/mo, no broker's fee, avail Nov. 1, call 555-3489 evgs.

Advertisement for a house/condo for sale

Notes: The format of a for-sale ad varies from area to area. More or fewer words may be abbreviated, according to local custom and according to the per-line rate of your local newspaper's classified ads section. You would be best off to check comparable ads in your local paper (or, if the ad is for a *Pennysaver* or other specialty paper, check in that publication) to see what the local custom is and whether the ads typically begin with the number of rooms or with the area or street where the house/condo is located.

Be sure to include the number of rooms, number of bathrooms, location, asking price, your phone number, and the fact that the sale is "by owner" (so that the prospective buyer understands there will be no broker's fee).

Beyond that, since you want to make the house/condo sound as attractive as possible, include any special features or advantages, such as only ten years old, two-car garage, wood-burning fireplace, new carpets/tile floors/parquet floors, central air, new appliances, all appliances included, finished basement, wooded lot, terrace, swimming pool, huge living room, secluded, good schools, two blocks from the police station, walk to the bus stop/train station, convenient to shopping.

If the house is a "handyman's special" (in need of a lot of fixing up), say so. As long as it's priced accordingly, you'll attract the people who are willing to invest "sweat equity" in lieu of more money—and you won't waste your time with people who aren't willing to take on such a project and aren't going to buy it.

If the price is "firm" (you aren't willing to negotiate), say that too. But it's better to ask a little more than you want and leave yourself some bargaining room. Most people love to think they got a bargain, and many simply aren't willing to buy a house for the asking price.

You may also want to mention the age and/or style of the house. ✎

Here's a sample ad, with typical abbreviations (remember, though, that these vary from area to area):

Montevideo Ln, 3 bdrms/2 bath, den w/sep entr (suit. home ofc), family rm, Tudor-style, 2-car gar, fin bsmt, all appls, central a/c, new carpets, wooded lot, secluded, grt schools, well cared-for, $200,000, by owner, 555-3489 evgs.

Advertisement for a car for sale

Depending on how much money you want to spend on per-line charges for the ad, your ad could be as simple as:

'99 Chrys Concorde, lo mileage, mint condtn, $14,000, 555-9678, lv msg.

Notes: You may also want to include color, *one owner* (more applicable to an older car), *8 cyl, convert, anti-lock brakes, new batt,* and such information as *must sell—movg out of state* to explain why you want to sell the car if it's still almost-new and in good condition. This last piece of information reassures the prospective buyer that it's not necessarily a lemon.

Endorsements/Requests

Letter praising a product, service, or business establishment

To Whom It May Concern:

I am writing to let you know how delighted I am with your service. Two different technicians have come out regularly to service our house. They sprayed for bugs slowly, carefully, and in every suitable place. They were careful and methodical, and they answered all my questions. They showed up on time. They were respectful of our home and property.

Better yet, when we had an ant problem in the kitchen a couple of months ago, you sent around a (different) technician who sprayed, left ant bait traps, and made a second trip out a week later, without a word, when winged ants showed up in the den. He reassured me that they were not termites but carpenter ants, and that I did not need costly fumigation. (You also held true to your promise that these extra visits were included in your service and would not cost anything additional.)

Your office even called me back a week later to inquire if all was well and to make sure we were not having any further problems. Now, that's service!

Of course I will recommend your company to my friends, but I wanted to write you a letter as well, to let you know how pleased I am. Thank you!

Sincerely yours,

Letter praising a service provider

To Whom It May Concern:

I am writing in praise of one of your employees, who regularly goes the extra mile. Your technician, Mike Arnold, has had to come out to repair our stove three times now for three different problems.

From the extra time he took in stamping mud off his work boots to prevent tracking on my floors to the patience he had with my inquisitive five-year-old, he showed care and concern above and beyond what his job required. When I asked him a question concerning my refrigerator, and he didn't know the answer, he checked with someone at the shop and called me later with the answer.

When he saw that our stove tilted slightly, because of the floors in this old house, he got a piece of tile out of his truck and slid it under one of the stove's feet to help make the surface more level. He said he didn't want to think that a pot might slide off the stove and burn my son or me.

I don't know if your company has an Employee-of-the-Year award, but if you do, I hope Mr. Arnold will win it. He deserves it.

Sincerely yours,

Letter offering a volunteer position

Dear Anne,

As you know, the Greater Norwood Community League is getting ready to plan our annual fund-raiser. At the Board of Directors' meeting last night, we discussed the various sorts of events we have had in the past and decided that this year we need something different to stimulate more community-wide interest and carry us to our goal.

We need a dedicated committee, chaired by an inventive, diligent, motivated, creative person. You were the unanimous first choice of all the board members, and we're hoping you'll agree to chair the committee this year.

I don't have to tell you how important our organization's work is, or why our need for funds is greater this year than ever before. You've been a dedicated, hard-working member of the league for many years now; please say you'll agree to chair the committee this year.

Sincerely,

Letters of Thanks

For a charitable contribution

Dear Ms. Perry:

Thank you for your generous contribution. The piano you donated to our organization will be placed in one of our three shelters for battered and abused women. I'm sure it will bring many hours of enjoyment to women who have had too little happiness in their lives. It's people like you who help make this world a better place for the rest of us.

Again, a very large thank-you from those of us in the organization and from the women who will benefit from your generous gift.

Sincerely yours,

For help getting a job

Dear Mr. Honeywell:

I have just been offered the position with *[company name]* that you know I wanted. I believe that your letter of recommendation and the phone call you made on my behalf were instrumental in their choosing me, and so I'm writing to thank you. I want you to know how appreciative I am.

Sincerely yours,

For a letter of recommendation

Dear Ms. Morgan,

Thank you for the letter of reference you wrote on my behalf. I have been accepted to the college of my choice, and I believe that your letter of recommendation was instrumental in that acceptance. In the years ahead, I intend to make you, the others who went to bat for me, and of course my parents proud of me. But mostly, right now, I want you to know how appreciative I am.

Sincerely yours,

As a follow-up letter to a job interview

Dear Mr. LaFrance:

Thank you for giving me the opportunity to interview with you yesterday. I am very interested in the possibility of working at Consolidated. You painted a picture of a challenging position in a company that can offer many opportunities and interesting work, as well as a work environment that I believe I would enjoy.

If you require any further information from me, please don't hesitate to let me know. I look forward to learning of your decision. Again, thank you for your time yesterday.

Sincerely yours,

To a former employer

Dear Ms. Larkin:

Although I am no longer working at Wayside Widgets, I want you to know that I enjoyed my time there and will always think highly of you and the people I worked with at Wayside. Thank you for making my work experience a pleasure. I hope you understand that my decision to leave was not based on unhappiness with my work environment. I simply had the opportunity to further my career by making a strategic move./I wished/needed to move to another part of the country.

My best wishes to you for corporate prosperity and personal health and happiness.

Sincerely yours,

Correspondence
with Publishers

Letter covering a manuscript
submission or query

Notes: The purpose of a manuscript query letter—
whether it's for a book or an article—is to explain
your idea briefly, show the editor that there is a need
and a readership for your book/article, estimate how
long it would take you to finish writing it, and list
your previous writing credits, or at least the most
significant or relevant ones. The cover letter for the
complete manuscript also needs to sell the editor.

For a book, it's often a good idea to mention
any comparable books already in print and how
your book differs from them and is more salable.

For an article, enclose clips of your published
articles. For a book query, enclose three chapters or
the equivalent, and a table of contents or synopsis
of what the book is to include. ✐

Dear Ms. Luther:

Writers usually have no trouble finding the right words to write a letter, business or personal, or to say something that may be difficult or awkward. But many people would rather go to the dentist than write a condolence note, or face an IRS audit than have to tell a member of the car pool why she's being asked to find some other way to get to work.

That's the idea behind my book *I'm at a Loss for Words*. The target readers would include virtually every English-speaking adult who's not a professional wordsmith—and that's a large potential readership.

The only comparable book I am aware of is *Lifetime Encyclopedia of Letters*, which deals only with the written word, not spoken, and does not cover many of the circumstances my book covers.

I'm enclosing the table of contents and some samples from the book. The complete manuscript is available

[Or] I anticipate having the manuscript completed by *[date]*

[Or] I estimate it would take me *[length of time]* to complete the book after getting a contract.

My previous writing credits include *[list]*.

Sincerely yours,

Letter inquiring about the status of a manuscript (after at least three months)

Dear Mr. Spencer:

On *[date],* I sent to your attention three chapters plus a synopsis of my book, *Now What'll I Do?,* along with the requisite SASE. Although three months have elapsed, I have yet to receive a reply. Of course I am concerned that my submission may have gone astray in the mail. Did you ever receive it? Did you return it? Is the project still under consideration?

I would appreciate any information you can give me. I am enclosing a business-size SASE to facilitate your reply. Thank you in advance for your help.

Sincerely yours,

Communicating with Your Landlord or Service Provider by Letter

---

Notifying the landlord that you are not renewing your lease

Dear Mr. Solomon:

This is to advise you that we will not be renewing our lease on Apartment 2-A at 28 Elm Street. At the lease's termination, on the 30th of April, we will be vacating.

We are leaving the place in good order and will appreciate an expeditious return of our security deposit, which you can send to our new address: 129 Maple Street. Thank you in advance for that courtesy.

Sincerely yours,

Giving your landlord thirty days' notice

Dear Mr. Sullivan:

This is to advise you that we will be vacating Apartment 31 at 328 Grand Boulevard on the 30th of April. This letter will serve as the requisite thirty days' notice.

We are leaving the place in good order and will appreciate an expeditious return of our security deposit, which you can send to our new address: 11 Hialeah Drive. Thank you in advance for that courtesy.

Sincerely yours,

Withholding rent pending the solution of a problem

Dear Ms. Johnston:

This letter is to advise you that we are withholding payment of December's rent because you have yet to make the requested repairs on our apartment, Unit D at 230 Coolidge Street. To refresh your memory, here are the repairs we've requested: (1) the radiator in the second bedroom still doesn't give heat; (2) two of the burners on the stove still don't function; (3) the drain stopper on the bathtub still doesn't work; and (4) you have not repaired the ceiling in the living room.

As soon as these repairs are satisfactorily completed, we will forward payment in full.

Sincerely yours,

Refusing to pay a bill until
service is rendered properly

Dear Mr. Dafoe:

I have received your bill for house painting. However, the quality of the work done was inferior. There are globs of paint in some places; you missed spots in others. Splotches of wall paint are on the ceiling in several places. In total, the job is absolutely unacceptable.

I am withholding payment until the job is done satisfactorily. Please call me at work at 555-7693 to make arrangements for a mutually convenient day when you can do the work needed to make the job right, and I can be there to watch. When the job is done correctly, I'll pay you.

Sincerely,

Where There's a Will . . .

Dear Rich,

As you know, I was named as executor of Dad's estate. What you may not know is that you were named as one of the beneficiaries. When everything is settled, you'll be receiving a check, some pieces of art, and Dad's piano.

I'll let you know when I have a shipping date on the artwork and the piano. The check will arrive by certified mail.

Give my love to Beverlee and the kids.

Love,

Letter notifying someone outside the family that she is a beneficiary

Dear Melinda,

I'm one of Monica Grennan's daughters. Mother spoke of you often, and fondly. You may not have heard, but Mother passed away recently. As executrix of her estate, I'm letting you know there was a small bequest made to you in her will.

I wanted to make sure that you're still at the same address. When you confirm that you are, and after the estate is settled, I'll mail a check to you.

I hope this note finds you in good health. I look forward to hearing from you.

Sincerely yours,

Letter notifying a relative that he is not a beneficiary

Dear Anthony,

You're probably wondering about the terms of Uncle Lou's will. As executor, I need to let you know that he left half his estate to a "special friend" and the other half to charity. Nothing went to the nieces and nephews (or any other relatives).

Call me if you have any questions. If you don't have my office number, it's 555-2286.

Love,

Letter asking when an estate will be settled

Dear Aunt Helene,

How are you? I hope you are feeling better and not burdened down by the emotional strain of being Uncle Marty's executrix on top of coping with his death.

I don't want to add to that strain, but I was wondering approximately when the estate is likely to be settled. I have little experience with these matters, and I have no idea how long it usually takes (or even whether this particular situation is typical).

For all I know, a check was mailed several weeks ago, and it went astray in the mail. In fact, it was that concern that prompted me to write you. Uncle Marty had left me with the belief that I would be receiving something after his death, and I can't help worrying about mail perhaps being lost.

Again, I hope this finds you well and coping in your usual way. If you ever want to just talk, call me. I'd love to hear from you. I haven't called you only because I wouldn't want to call at an inopportune time. I can imagine your life must be a bit topsy-turvy at this point.

With love,

Letter explaining that a will has not yet been probated

Dear Louise,

I think you are aware you were named in my father's will. You may be wondering when to expect your bequest. I just wanted to explain to you that the will has not yet been probated, so none of the assets have been distributed.

I hope this will be accomplished in the next month, although that is not a promise, just an estimate. I'll keep you posted if there is a further significant delay.

All my best,

PART THREE
Strictly Business

Dismissal/Resignation

Conversation dismissing an employee

"John, I think you may have an idea why I've asked to talk to you. You know I haven't been happy with your performance lately. I've spoken to you about missing deadlines and generally sloppy work. I've also spoken to you about your habitual lateness. I was hoping these conversations would lead to some improvement in performance and attitude. Unfortunately, they haven't.

"Under the circumstances, John, I have no other recourse but to let you go. It's never easy to terminate someone's employment, but I have no choice. Your position here will end on the fourteenth of this month.

[Or] Your dismissal is effective immediately; here's a check for two weeks' severance.

"I'm sorry it had to come to this, but that's the way it has to be. I wish you the best of luck in your future endeavors."

Letter dismissing an employee

Dear Lana:

This isn't an easy letter to write, but you know I haven't been happy with your performance lately. I've spoken to you about missing deadlines and sloppy work. I've also spoken to you about your habitual lateness. I had hoped these conversations would lead to some improvement in performance and attitude. Unfortunately, they haven't.

Under the circumstances, I have no other recourse but to let you go. It's never easy to terminate someone's employment, but I have no choice. Your position here will end on the fourteenth of this month.

[Or] Your dismissal is effective immediately; enclosed is a check for two weeks' severance.

I wish you the best of luck in your future endeavors.

Sincerely yours,

Verbal resignation from a job

"Mr. Edwards, I hope this isn't inconvenient for you, but I'm giving you my two weeks' notice. I've found another position, and I'll be leaving the company as of the seventeenth. If you would like me to help train my replacement before I leave, I'll be happy to do that. My final date has to be the seventeenth, however, since I start my new position the following Monday. Best of luck to you."

Letter of resignation

Dear Ms. Finch:

Effective the twenty-second of this month, I will no longer be working for XYZ Company. I have accepted an employment offer elsewhere. I hope that giving you two weeks' notice will enable you to hire a replacement for me. If you want me to help train my replacement, I'll be happy to do that, of course. I wish you and XYZ the best of luck and success.

Sincerely yours,

Letter of recommendation
for an acceptable employee

To Whom It May Concern:

It is my pleasure to recommend Ben Darwin to you. In the three years he has been in our employ, he has shown himself to be a person who *[use any of the following that apply, and/or add others of your own choosing that are applicable]* follows directions well, takes the initiative, is creative, has the company's interests at heart, has a good working relationship with his fellow employees, has suggested many improvements for the benefit of the company, is a great team player, is extremely bright, is very motivated, is very conscious of the bottom line.

We are sorry to lose him, but I understand that his opportunities here are limited and that a person of his talents naturally wants to go where he has more avenues for career growth *[or]* where he can be more adequately compensated for his skills/intelligence.

If you have any further questions, please don't hesitate to call or write me, but I unhesitatingly commend Ben Darwin to you. Our loss will be your gain.

Sincerely,

Letter of recommendation for an unacceptable employee

Notes: This kind of recommendation is known as "damning with faint praise." You're reluctant to bluntly say that your employee did minimal work, that he and timeliness didn't even have a nodding acquaintance, that he gave company supplies a much-needed change of scene (by taking them home for his personal use), that his talent for lying qualifies him as a fiction writer, and that his penchant for water cooler gossip has made him eligible for the Most Popular Employee to Kill Valuable Time With. So you write a letter filled with positive things you can say honestly, but you make it so insipid that it's obvious you aren't *really* recommending him at all.

To Whom It May Concern:

Bob Craft has been in our employ for three years now. He performs his work adequately, is reasonably conscientious about showing up on time, has not made any major errors, and gets along with his fellow employees.

Sincerely yours,

Job Seeking/Hiring

Crafting a resume with minimal work experience

Notes: Without some heavy-duty lying, you aren't going to fool prospective employers into thinking you have vast work experience, no matter how creative your resume. But you can take life experiences and make them work to your advantage if you have the right kind of things to draw upon.

For instance, if you're newly graduated from college or high school, do you have part-time or after-school work you can show on your resume? Make the most of it. Without lying, you can still show it in the most favorable light possible, explaining that you shouldered responsibility, demonstrated leadership skills or were good at following directions, were a good team player, and perhaps thought of ways to cut costs or do your job more efficiently.

Either a recent grad or a former stay-at-home mom or dad might have performed organizational work that demonstrates skills, abilities, and other qualities that are marketable in the work force. I'm certainly not suggesting you point out that you sold more Girl Scout cookies than any other Brownie in your troop, but what about more recent organizational or similar experience?

Were you class president or president of a club or other organization? Have you been head of the PTA or of a committee within it? Did you take charge of publicity for your neighborhood improvement organization? Did you coordinate an event for your church or synagogue? Make the most of your experience, whatever it's been. Play it up without actually lying. Political candidates know the difference between fraudulent claims and mere "puffing"—you can learn it, too.

Even if your only work experience has been flipping burgers or delivering pizza, you've demonstrated a desirable work ethic if you showed up faithfully and worked hard. After all, everyone has to start somewhere—and you're certainly not applying for a position as corporate CEO.

Play up whatever work experience you can, whatever other life experience you've had that demonstrates skills and/or desirable qualities, and of course your education. Don't lie, but do show yourself in your most favorable light. After all, if you don't, who's going to?! ✏️

Letter responding to a help-wanted ad

To Whom It May Concern:

I hope the enclosed resume will intrigue you as much as your ad has intrigued me. I believe that my *[if one of the following does not apply, omit it]* skills, education, and past experience qualify me for the position you're looking to fill, and I would like to discuss this with you further. I hope to hear from you soon.

Sincerely yours,

Resume cover letter for a known position

To Whom It May Concern:

I understand *[add if applicable]* from your employee Ken Smith that you are currently seeking an engineer. I am interested in a better position than my present one *[or]* I am available, and I would like to interview with you for the opening you have. I believe that my resume, which is enclosed, will show that I am well qualified.

I hope to hear from you soon.

Sincerely yours,

Resume cover letter (not sent in response to a job opening)

To Whom It May Concern:

Although I do not know whether you currently need a plant safety manager *[or]* a person with my skills and experience, I am enclosing my resume in case you have a suitable opening. If you do not have an immediate opening, please keep my resume on file for future reference.

[Use some version of whichever of the following four paragraphs is applicable:]

> Until recently I was employed by XYZ Company, as you'll see on my resume.

> I am currently employed, but I am seeking better pay/a greater challenge/a position in which I can better use my skills and my education.

> I am a recent college graduate, but as my resume shows, I worked part-time throughout my undergraduate years.

> I am currently employed but am seeking evening work for additional income.

Thank you for giving my resume consideration.
Sincerely yours,

Nontraditional letter requesting employment (no resume)

To Whom It May Concern:

Of all the collections people applying for the position you have available, why should you hire *me*? I'll give you several reasons:

1. If I have the audacity to apply for the job, I'm not going to be intimidated by people on the phone.
2. If I have the creativity to write a letter like this, I'm going to apply creativity to the job, too.
3. Since I've never done this type of work before, you can train me to do it *your* way (without first having to *un*train some previous employer's methods that may be at odds with your way of doing things).
4. Since I'm a recent graduate, I'm still young and energetic, ambitious and in need of a job, and will therefore work hard for you.

I am a graduate of *[state college and degree, or high school if not a college grad]* and my past work experience includes *[list summer jobs, after-school work—anything reasonable you can show]*.

Am I the perfect person to fill the opening you have? You'll never know until you interview me. You can reach me at 555-6730.

Thank you for your consideration.

Sincerely yours,

Letter requesting further information from a job applicant

Dear Ms. Monroe:

With reference to your job application, your background gives us some interest in you, but there are several people we are considering. We would appreciate it if you would supply us with the following information:

1. Why did you leave ABC Worldwide?
2. What was your major in college?
3. Where were you employed from 1987 to 1989?

We would also like to know what salary range you are hoping for.

Faxing your answers to us would facilitate matters. The sooner we have the information we need, the sooner we can make an informed choice. Thank you.

Sincerely yours,

Letter requesting a reference
for a job applicant

Dear Ms. Kittredge:

Trey Amberson has applied for employment with our company. He has given your name as a reference. We would appreciate any information you believe would be of interest to us in this connection. Of course, we will keep your reply confidential.

I am enclosing a self-addressed, stamped envelope to facilitate your response. Thank you in advance for your response.

Sincerely yours,

Collections/Payments/ Price Quotes

Collection letter, polite first notice

Dear Mr. Caruthers:

Although we're sure it's just an oversight, our invoice of May 31 for $356.78 remains unpaid. Won't you please take a moment now to send out a check?

Thank you very much,

Collection letter, firm second notice

Dear Ms. Lewis:

Our invoice to you dated April 30, in the amount of $798.87, remains unpaid, despite a polite reminder sent two weeks ago. The account is now nearly sixty days past due. Payment must be made immediately or your credit privileges will be suspended and the account turned over for collection.

Please give this your immediate attention!

Sincerely yours,

Collection letter, humorous

Dear Mr. Kenney:

In a perfect world—

- The right politicians would always get elected
- People could sleep as late as they wanted every day
- Planes would always depart and arrive on time
- Furniture would be given away

But unfortunately, this is a far-from-perfect world. The wrong person often seems to get elected. Most of us need to get up before we're ready in order to be at work on time. Airlines are notoriously tardy. And our product is not free.

So I find myself with the unpleasant task of reminding you that when we sold you that living room set on November 10, you signed an agreement to pay $181.34 a month until it was paid off. We have yet to receive your December payment.

Maybe you've been so busy that you overlooked our book of payment coupons when it arrived by mail? Whatever the reason, please take a minute to send us that check now. Thank you.

Sincerely yours,

Letter stating that continued delinquencies will damage creditworthiness

Dear Ms. Harris:

Your company has been consistently late in paying our invoices. At this point you are not only jeopardizing your credit standing with us, you are risking having us report this delinquency to the credit bureaus. I'm sure you're aware this could seriously damage your creditworthiness in the future.

Won't you please rectify this problem by paying all our invoices in a timely manner? Thank you.

Sincerely yours,

Letter requesting credit information

Dear Mr. Edwards:

Your company has requested credit from our company, but Dun & Bradstreet has no credit information available for you. To help us reach a decision, we need the following information:

- Length of time your company has been in business
- Bank and branch where your account is located, and the account number
- The names and addresses of other firms with whom you have established credit

Sincerely yours,

Letter requesting a credit reference

Dear Ms. Larrabee:

Jon DeVito of Ace Optical recently applied for credit with us and gave your company's name as a reference. He says that he has been doing business on a credit basis with your firm. We would appreciate your sharing any relevant information with us. We are especially interested in how long Ace has done business on credit with you and how promptly they pay, as well as any other significant information such as their credit limit with you.

Naturally, your reply will be kept confidential.

I am enclosing a stamped, self-addressed envelope to facilitate your reply. Thank you in advance for your help.

Sincerely yours,

Letter declining credit but offering to do business on a cash basis

Dear Mr. Walters:

With regard to your request to establish credit with us, we must respectfully decline at this time. Of course, we would be happy to do business on a cash basis, however. We would also be willing to reconsider the credit question after six months of doing business together.

I hope this will be the beginning of a mutually satisfactory business relationship.

Sincerely yours,

Letter supplying a price quote

Dear Ms. Montrose:

Thank you for your request for a price quote for 600 widgets shipped F.O.B. Atlanta. In that quantity, the per-unit cost would be $10.87, exclusive of shipping costs. If you were interested in buying 1,000 at a time, there would be a significant savings; the per-unit cost (again exclusive of shipping) would be $10.14.

Our usual method of shipping is UPS. We ship within three days of receiving an order. If you have any further questions, please don't hesitate to contact me. I hope I can look forward to doing business with you.

Sincerely yours,

Letter adjusting a price quote

Dear Ms. Montrose:

I recently sent you a price quote for 600 widgets shipped F.O.B. Atlanta. At the time, I stated the per-unit cost would be $10.87, exclusive of shipping costs. I added that if you were interested in buying 1,000 at a time, the per-unit cost (again exclusive of shipping) would be $10.14.

Since then, our cost for sprockets for the widgets has increased dramatically, and we are forced to raise our prices effective March 1st. Of course we will honor any orders we receive before that date at the price I quoted you in my letter last week. After March 1st, however, the per-unit price for 600 widgets will be $10.99; in orders of 1,000, it will be $10.27.

If you have any further questions, please don't hesitate to contact me.

Sincerely yours,

Letter seeking quotes from prospective vendors

To Whom It May Concern:

Our company is seeking quotes from vendors for (1) ½-inch widgets and (2) large round sprockets.

We would like to know the cost per unit both for low-quantity orders and for orders of 1,000 and 10,000. Also advise what your terms are, how you ship, and how quickly you ship.

Thank you for your help.

Sincerely yours,

Letter seeking quotes on office space

To Whom It May Concern:

XYZ Company is seeking larger quarters. We need approximately 1,000 square feet of air-conditioned space, preferably at street level, with adequate electrical outlets. We would like to remain in the same general area.

Do you have any office space that would fit our needs? We would appreciate answers to the following questions:

1. How much is the rent?
2. When is it available for occupancy?
3. How long a lease are you offering?

Please reply to the fax number given above. No phone calls, please. Thank you.

Sincerely yours,

Thanks/Appreciation/Goodwill

Customer appreciation letter

Dear Mr. Bonaventura:

Customers like you make it a pleasure to be in this business. You've been a faithful customer for three years now, and you always pay your bills on time. We appreciate your loyalty as well as your promptness in payment.

Everyone likes feeling appreciated, and we just wanted to let you know that we appreciate your business and your way of doing business.

[Include this paragraph if applicable] We would like to show our appreciation with something more concrete than words, however, so please take 5 percent off the cost of your next order from us. It's our way of saying thank-you. You deserve it!

With thanks,

Letter to a former customer

Dear Mr. Ormond:

It's been over half a year since we heard from you. Did we do something to displease you? Did we somehow lose your trust?

I like to think that one of the advantages of dealing with a smaller company like ours is that you're not just an order number to us . . . and we're not just a faceless corporation to you. So if we've done something that put us in the doghouse, please tell me.

I won't embarrass you by calling and asking, but if we've failed you, I'd really appreciate it if you'd call me and tell me what happened. (How can we serve our customers well if we don't know when we're not doing our best?)

And—whether we've disappointed you or not—I certainly hope we'll be hearing from you again.

Sincerely yours,

Letter thanking an employee
for a job well done

Dear Lisa,

Too many employers think a Christmas bonus is enough of a thank-you when an employee does her job well, but I still believe in the value of communication. You're one of the reasons this company runs as smoothly as it does, because you straighten out problems as soon as they arise.

That's why I'm taking this occasion to say thank-you for a job well done every day. I don't want you to think your value to the company and your contribution to our operation are going unnoticed. Thank you, Lisa.

Appreciatively,

Letter thanking an employee for his performance on a specific project

Dear Burt,

We couldn't have done it without you. The MacIver project was a real thorn in everyone's side, but you pulled the whole thing together. You provided everything from the creative inspiration that made it possible to the organizational know-how that brought it in on time despite the client's unrealistic deadlines.

Of course my gratitude will be reflected in your Christmas bonus, but I didn't want to wait until Christmas to express how much I appreciate your contribution.

Thanks again, Burt. Well done!

Appreciatively,

Letter thanking a job applicant for interviewing

Dear Ms. Allorca:

Thank you for taking your time to interview at XYZ Company. Although we were impressed with you, we spoke with a number of fine candidates and have ultimately decided on one of the other applicants. I wish you the best of luck in your search for the right position. *[If applicable, add:]* I'm sure that with your qualifications, something good will come along soon.

Sincerely yours,

Letter acknowledging the receipt of a resume, when you have no openings

Dear Mr. Harcourt:

Thank you for sending us your resume. Although you appear very well qualified, we have no openings at present *[or]* we have no openings at present for which you are suited.

We would like to keep your resume on file. If anything suitable comes up in the reasonable future, we'll be in touch. Thanks for your interest in Wayside Widgets.

Sincerely yours,

Letter to a dissatisfied customer

Dear Ms. Matewski,

I appreciate receiving your letter of complaint, although I am troubled by it. It disturbs me to think that we've let a valued customer down.

Thank you for taking the time to write and tell us. If you hadn't written us, we would never have known that anything was wrong.

Please rest assured I am taking steps to correct the conditions you mentioned. *[Add if appropriate:]* And to put our money where our corporate mouth is, I'm enclosing a coupon for 10 percent off on your next purchase/order/dinner in our restaurant/print job/_____. At XYZ, every customer/client/patron is important to us.

Thank you again for bringing the situation to my attention. We always welcome customer feedback! How else can we know if we're doing a good job! Thank you.

Sincerely yours,

Letter to a coworker who lost out to you for a promotion

Dear John,

You certainly merit recognition for your hard work, and it's my hope that very soon you'll get the promotion that you deserve. In the meantime, I hope that there is no rancor over my having been named to the new post, and that I can count on your support as we work together for the good of the company/foundation/organization.

Sincerely,

Letter congratulating a coworker who received a promotion over you

Dear Sara,

Congratulations on being made manager of plant operations. I'm sure you'll do a fine job. Although we were each hoping to get that promotion, you know you can count on me to be supportive. Again, congratulations.

Sincerely,

Customer Relations

Letter responding to a request for information

Dear Ms. Edwards:

I am pleased to be able to supply you with the information you requested in your letter of August 4th:

[Provide information or say] I am enclosing a brochure/fact sheet/spec sheet that answers all the questions you asked.

If you have any further questions, please don't hesitate to call me. It will be my pleasure to help you.

Sincerely yours,

Letter refusing to supply requested information

Dear Mr. Nastri:

Thank you for your letter of May 9th, requesting information. Unfortunately, the information you want simply isn't available. *[Or]* I'm sorry to tell you I cannot give you the information you are requesting because it would violate our privacy policy. I regret being unable to help you in this matter, but if there is anything further you would like to know, or any other way in which I can be of help, please ask.

Sincerely yours,

Letter declining to continue doing business with a client

Dear Ms. Waxworth:

In the three years this firm has serviced your accounting needs, I've always felt that we've failed to live up to your expectations. Your displeasure has become evident your many phone calls to our staff, often conducted in a loud and angry voice. The incident last Thursday was just one more in a long series.

At this point, I think that it would be best if you sought another accountancy practice to handle your needs.

Please accept my best wishes for continuing success in your endeavors.

Sincerely yours,

Letter refusing to share credit information

Dear Mr. Lowe:

With regard to your inquiry concerning Mr. Josiah Abercrombie, it is not our company policy to divulge that information. Therefore we must respectfully decline to answer your questions.

Sincerely yours,

Letter asking a third party to supply a credit reference to a vendor

Dear Ms. Franklin:

You will be receiving correspondence from ABC Amalgamated in the near future, if you haven't already. The letter will be a request for credit information regarding our firm. We would appreciate your answering their questions, as we have applied to do business with them on a credit basis.

Thank you very much for your cooperation.

Sincerely yours,

Letter refusing to provide information about your company

Dear Mr. Manton:

I am in receipt of your letter of June 28th, in which you ask a number of questions about our company. It is not our policy to divulge that particular information, so I must respectfully decline to answer.

Sincerely yours,

Letter apologizing for delayed shipping

Dear Ms. LaTerre:

Your order of April 12th (your P.O. #348) should have been shipped today, but realistically it may take another five days.

Unfortunately, the machinery at our plant broke down, and we have been waiting for a replacement part. Although we anticipate that repairs will be completed today, production is behind schedule and orders are backlogged.

We are doing everything we can to beat that projected five-day delay. If we can ship sooner, we certainly will, but I don't want to disappoint you a second time by making a promise I may not be able to keep. Your patience during this difficult time is greatly appreciated.

Sincerely yours,

Letter apologizing for a performance delay (reason apparent)

Dear Mr. Rangell:

Due to the U.P.S. strike, we have not yet received a new supply of blue ink and do not have enough for the press run of your forms. Therefore, we will not be able to make delivery by Friday as promised.

We have asked our supplier to arrange for another method of shipping and hope to have the forms printed and delivered to you shortly after the date promised. Please bear with us during these extenuating circumstances, which are beyond our control.

Thank you for your patience and understanding.

Sincerely yours,

Letter apologizing for a performance delay (reason not apparent)

Dear Ms. Henderson:

Due to a computer problem here in our office, I will not have the tax forms completed and ready for our scheduled meeting on January 8 at 10 A.M. I have rescheduled our meeting for January 11 at the same time, subject to your approval.

I am confident the computer will be functioning properly and the forms will be completed by then. I am committed to working late every evening till the work backlog has been disposed of, and I apologize for any inconvenience this rescheduling and delay may cause you. Rest assured, though, you will have the forms in ample time to review them and send them in.

If January 11 at 10 A.M. is not convenient for you, please call my office to arrange another time; otherwise, you don't need to do anything.

Thank you for your patience and understanding.

Sincerely yours,

Cute letter apologizing for an error

Dear Ms. Larrabee:

Oops, we goofed!

If "to err is human," then perhaps computers are human after all. It was a computer error that caused the erroneous $100 charge to be posted to your account.

[Or]

If "to err is human," then you must know that this office is still in human hands, because we certainly erred when we posted that incorrect $100 charge to your account.

But the important thing isn't how it got there; the important thing is that it has been removed. We have egg on our faces (and it's hard to work with yolk dripping from your eyebrows!), but we promise to be extra-careful that this sort of thing doesn't happen again.

Sincerely yours,

Formal letter apologizing for an error

Dear Mr. Hanneford:

We regret our billing error of September 30, in which we showed a past due item that in fact you had paid promptly the month before. I want to reassure you that we have corrected our records, that the payment has been properly posted, that you are not reflected as a delinquent payer, and that we are very aware of your spotless payment record.

We will be vigilant in our efforts to keep this sort of error from recurring. And again, we apologize.

Sincerely yours,

Letter thanking a customer
for an early payment

Dear Ms. Halloran:

It is a pleasure to do business with a customer who pays her bills not only consistently on time but early. As a way of saying thank-you, we are offering to increase your credit limit on future purchases/orders to $____.

Additionally, if you ever need a credit reference, it would be our pleasure to be a reference for you.

Thank you again for the estimable manner in which you pay your bills.

Sincerely yours,

Letter declining a business gift

Dear Ed:

Thank you so much for the bottle of single malt scotch you sent me. I would love to accept it, but it is against the principles of this company to accept business gifts from clients or prospective clients.

I truly appreciate your generosity, but please understand my position in having to return the scotch.

Sincerely yours,

Rental Space

Letter advising a tenant her lease will not be renewed

Dear Ms. Keeler:

I will not be able to renew your lease when it expires on April 30, because I am planning to do extensive remodeling of the building/ my daughter is interested in occupying the garage apartment in the near future/ of the problems we have had during your tenancy.

I believe that I am giving you adequate notice so you can find other accommodations. After you vacate, we will inspect the premises. If all is found in order, we will send a refund of your security deposit.

Thank you for your cooperation.

Sincerely yours,

Letter advising a tenant of a partial/ non-refund of a security deposit

Dear Mr. Alonzo:

This is to advise you that we are not refunding your security deposit/that we are enclosing only a partial refund of your security deposit. The reason[s] for the non-refund/partial refund is/are:

[List damages or other conditions for which you are withholding all or part of the deposit.]

This is in accordance with the terms of your lease.

Sincerely yours,

Letter asking a tenant to vacate in thirty days

Dear Ms. Mallinor:

I would like you to vacate the premises by April 30 because I plan to do extensive remodeling of the building/my daughter is interested in occupying the garage apartment in the near future/of the past problems we have had regarding timely payment of your rent. Please consider this letter as your thirty-day notice.

Thank you for your cooperation.

After you vacate, we will inspect the premises. If all is found in order, we will send a refund of your security deposit.

Sincerely yours,

Politics

Political campaign letter from an incumbent

Dear Neighbor,

What are two of the most gratifying words a politician can hear (besides "Thank you")? We think they might be, "Well done!" Your councilwoman, Mary Lou Abernathy, hears those words often from voters in her district who appreciate the job she's done—and done well—for them.

If you're appreciative that local taxes have actually gone down . . . if you're happy that the city emergency response system has a new ambulance . . . if you like the new petting zoo for kids . . . if you're glad that topless bars have been zoned out of the downtown area . . . if you like the new regulations holding restaurants to stricter health standards . . . thank Mary Lou. She voted on the right side of all these issues and helped bring about these changes.

And if you *really* want to help Mary Lou, there are two great ways to do it:

1. Vote for her in the elections this November.
2. Send in a campaign contribution to help her get re-elected.

A contribution card is enclosed. Please fill it out and give whatever you can afford. But even if you don't contribute, please remember to show up at the polls on November 9th and vote for Mary Lou Abernathy. Tell her "Well done!" by casting your vote for her. And give her a chance to go on doing great things for our city!

Political campaign letter from a non-incumbent

Dear Neighbor,

What time is it when crime is up for the third straight year in a row? What time is it when the city doesn't offer its kids any organized after-school activities . . . when three accidents at the city's ice rink point to poor maintenance on the part of the Parks Department . . . when property values around town are going down . . . when the politicians are getting complacent?

What time is it? *It's time for a change.*

It's time for a change—and it's time to elect Nora Pariente to the city council. Nora's a local lawyer . . . and a local mom. She's a fighter . . . and a diplomat. She's caring . . . and she's relentless. Nora knows how to get things done. She cares about the same things you do. With Nora in the city council, we can make our city great again. Wouldn't you like to be proud of the place where you live? Wouldn't you like to know the home you've invested money—and hard work, and love—into is worth *more* than when you bought it, not *less?*

Then vote for Nora Pariente on November 9. Thank you for your support. See you at the polls on the 9th!

Letter congratulating a rival candidate

Dear Ray,

Congratulations on winning the city council seat/presidency of the organization/*[other]*. I'm sure you'll do a fine job. Despite the fact that we were rivals for the position, you know you'll have my support in the year[s] ahead.

Sincerely,

PART FOUR
Speeches and Toasts

Accepting an honor

"Thank you very much . . . and thank you, all, for being here to share this moment of honor with me. Although this is a very proud occasion for me, my sense of pride is tempered by the knowledge that I didn't accomplish this on my own.

"All the work I've done, all the time I've given to this great organization has been matched by the hours, the ideas, and the hard work of so many other members who devoted brain power and muscle power, who gave up free time and family time, to do more than their share for this wonderful club/cause of ours.

"If I have to single out just a few names to recognize for contributions way above and beyond, I'd certainly mention *[names]*. But there are others I haven't mentioned, and I don't mean to slight them by leaving them out. We're all in this together, and I truly appreciate the contributions of everyone—every one of *you*.

[If applicable, add]

"I also want to thank my family. Every time I was at a meeting, an event, a committee meeting, I wasn't at home. Every time I was working for the good of *[name of organization]*, I *wasn't* spending time with my family. So they've contributed as well. *[If applicable, add:]* They've helped in more concrete ways, too: *[give examples of work done by family members]*.

"I know that I'll continue to work hard for *[name of organization],* and I know that you'll continue to join me. Once again, thank you all!"

Passing the torch to the next president of your organization

"Today is an end and a beginning. It's been a pleasure and an honor to be president of this organization for the last year. I leave the presidency with some sorrow, but in very capable hands.

"*[Name]* will be a very good president, I'm confident, and it gives me pleasure to know that *[name of organization]* will be in her hands.

"I want to thank all the people who helped make the achievements of my presidency possible. I can't name everyone, but I especially want to thank *[names]* for everything they've done to help me make *[name of organization]* the great organization that it is. *[Add if applicable]* I also want to thank my family, *[names]*, for standing behind me and understanding when I had meetings and other work for *[name of organization]* that took large chunks of time out of my schedule, time I should have been spending with them.

"Now it's *[name of incoming president]*'s turn. I know she will be a gifted leader. Together we will work for this great club/cause and accomplish more than ever before.

"Ladies and gentlemen, I give you our next president, *[name]*."

Delivering a eulogy

"I've come here not to mourn a death but to celebrate a life. Yes, we are all going to miss *[name]*. We are going to miss him very much, in fact. How could we not miss someone who was a loving *[whichever one(s) is/are applicable]* son/daughter/mother/father/wife/husband/sister/brother, _____ not to mention friend? *[Add whichever is/are applicable]* How could we not miss someone who was so active in his church/synagogue? How could we not miss someone who was so involved in *[name(s) of organizations/charities/clubs]*? How could we not miss someone who was so well liked by his neighbors and friends?

"But it is *because* he was so involved, was so well liked, and did so much that I want today to celebrate his life as much as mourn his death. His family is going to miss him especially—his wife *[name]*, his children *[names],* and also *[other relatives—relationships and names]*.

"His friends are going to miss him too . . . but they will always remember what a true friend, what a giving friend, what a wonderful friend he was.

A friend who always had time for others. A friend who could make others laugh. A friend who was a pleasure to be with. A friend who cared.

[If applicable, add]

"The people who worked with/worked for/did business with him will miss him too. How could they feel otherwise, with a person like *[name]*?

"His death was a great shock, and *[or]* His death was not a big surprise, but still it is a huge loss. But I ask you today to remember *[name]* as you will always want to remember him—alive and involved—and be happy for all the years we had to enjoy him instead of crying now for all the years we will be without him.

"Do you want to know how I'll remember *[name]*? *[Relate one typical or outstanding incident or else describe the deceased as he most typically was—in looks or in activity.]*

"And so let's try not to shed too many tears today—although some are unavoidable. Let's celebrate *[name]*, the person, his life, and let's remember the good times, the happy times, the everyday times, and be glad for all the years we had with him. Farewell, *[name]*, you were a wonderful person."

Toasting a milestone birthday

"I don't have to tell you why we're here today. Obviously, we're here to celebrate *[name]*'s birthday—and not just any birthday but a special birthday. But more than that, I don't have to tell you why *[name]*'s friends and family wanted to make an occasion out of this birthday, why we've gathered honor *[name]*: *[name]* is a very special person.

"A devoted mother/daughter/sister/*[other]*, equally loyal as a friend, *[name]* is someone we can count on, someone who'll always be there for us, and someone we all enjoy being with. She's *[list a few applicable adjectives such as:]* loyal, fun loving, studious, serious, family-oriented, caring, deeply religious, highly ethical, committed, hard working, devoted, kind, compassionate.

"So here's a toast to *[name]*. May your next *[same number as whatever birthday this is]* years be even happier, more enjoyable, and more productive than these *[number of this birthday]* have been. May you enjoy them in good health, in happiness, and surrounded by those you care about. May every day be better than the one before. And may life never let you down!"

Toasting an engagement

"Here's to *[names of engaged couple]*, two wonderful people whose engagement we're celebrating tonight. In just *[length of time till wedding]*, we'll be toasting them again as bride and groom, but right now they're embarking on exciting times as they prepare for what will probably be the most important day of their lives.

"May this be the beginning of a wonderful, satisfying, extremely happy marriage, one blessed with everything you two hope for, one that brings you comfort, joy, companionship, satisfaction, and great pleasure. May you enjoy it in good health, in a generous measure of prosperity, and surrounded by family you love and friends who care about you—just as we surround you tonight.

"Here's to you, *[names]*, and may all your deepest wishes and wildest dreams come true."

Toasting a wedding

"*[Names of bride and groom],* we're all gathered here to wish you well as you start out on the most exciting adventure life can offer—your marriage. You've chosen each other, and we all know why. You're both wonderful people, and we wish you nothing but the best life can bring.

"We wish you peace and contentment, joy and excitement, and the fulfillment of every one of your dreams, both for your life together and for your lives as individuals, for the greater your individual contentment, the easier it will be to live in happiness and harmony together.

"Whatever you do in your life together, may you do it well and with great satisfaction. May you live in your dream house, surrounded by those you love, and enjoy a more-than-average measure of prosperity, too. And, of course, may you both enjoy great good health.

"May your disagreements be minor and your squabbles be settled quickly. May your mutual interests grow and your satisfactions be many. May more than your fair share of your dreams be fulfilled.

"And may we all gather together again fifty years from now to toast you on your golden anniversary, and may you then be every bit as much in love with each other as you are now . . . and looking forward to the years still ahead as tonight you look forward to the wonderful future that awaits you. I drink to your happiness and to a long and satisfying marriage. Here's to you, *[names]*."

Toasting the retirement of an employee

"We're here tonight to honor *[name]*, but as much as we're happy for him on the milestone occasion, we're all a little sad too, because he won't be working with us anymore.

"It's been my pleasure—it's been a pleasure for all of us—to have *[name]* working for us. *[Name]* has been a dedicated employee, a tireless worker, a good friend to his fellow workers, and someone we could all count on.

"Tonight we wish you well, *[name]*, as you go on to the next phase of your life. Whether you fill your retirement years with hobbies, with travel, with volunteer work, or just with mellowing out and slowing down, we wish you the satisfaction and contentment you've certainly earned. We hope that the years ahead are filled with whatever you want them to hold, that you enjoy them surrounded by family and friends, and that you find great joy or inner peace, excitement or contentment . . . whatever it is you want for yourself.

"We wish you a long stretch of satisfying years ahead of you. Enjoy them . . . and above all, enjoy them in good health!"

Toasting the retirement of a friend

"We're all here tonight to wish *[name]* well on the occasion of her retirement. As her friend, I'm very happy to know she's finally going to have more time for the things she enjoys doing in her leisure hours: *[name some of the retiree's hobbies if applicable],* being with family, and—of course—being with friends.

"Of course, if she spends too much time *[select one most applicable:]* reading/fishing/crocheting/building models/*[other]*, she may have to go back to work to support her book/lure/wool/*[other]* habit!

"But *[name]*, we're here tonight to toast you, not just to tease you. You've given a good part of yourself to *[name of company]*, and now it's time for life to give back to you in return. Whether you spend those years traveling or playing/learning chess, volunteering or just spending more time with family and friends, I hope—we all hope—you'll enjoy whatever you do.

"Make those years meaningful; make them count. Enjoy yourself in whatever ways please you the most. Let's all drink to that, and to you, *[name],* my friend!"

Honoring a friend for good works

"We all know why we're here tonight . . . to honor *[name]*, a person who richly deserves to have an evening in his honor. What has he done? Oh, nothing much . . . unless you want to count *[list all the accomplishments directly related to the topic of that evening's honor, such as twenty years of selfless work for a charity or spearheading a fundraising drive that took an organization over the top, or being the motivational force behind getting a new library built]*. And that's just what he's being honored for this evening. Let's not forget that *[name]* is/has accomplished *[list some or all of his other recent credits/accomplishments]*.

"On top of that, *[name]* has raised/is raising a family, *[and/or]* is a wonderful son to his parents/father/mother, has long been an active and involved member of our community in general, and *[add any other reasonable facts that are to the honoree's credit even if they're not worthy of honor by themselves, such as teaching, being active in his church/synagogue, being a respected local businessperson, etc.]*.

"I am also deeply privileged to call this person

my friend. And when you have *[name]* for a friend, you have someone you can count on. You have a friend for life.

"All of us here who know and care about *[name]* have been touched by him in some way or other . . . or in many ways. If we've worked shoulder to shoulder with him, we know his capacity for tireless work and devotion to a cause/organization/project he cares about. If we can count him as a personal friend, we're truly enriched. In any case, we're all the beneficiaries of his remarkable efforts on behalf of *[name of cause/organization/project]*.

"And so, *[name]*, we salute you tonight. And we [raise our glasses to you and] wish you the same measure of satisfaction from life that we have all gotten from our association with you and that *[project/cause/organization]* has gotten from your work in its behalf. May you be as enriched by life as we all are by knowing you, and may life pay you back as fully as you deserve."

Acknowledging a friend who has been elected to office or promoted at work

"*[Name],* it's a privilege for me to be able to stand here and honor you tonight, because I can't think of anyone more deserving. You know—we all know—why we're here tonight, but I wonder if everyone present knows just what an exemplary all-around life you live. Yes, we're here because *[give reason for tonight's honor]*, but, *[name]*, you also are *[say any or all of the below that are applicable, and add any others you think of]* a wonderful family person, a very involved citizen in your community, active in your church/synagogue, very involved in various civic organizations, a mainstay at work, and _____.

"Let me give one example of why you're being honored tonight—just in case there's anyone here who doesn't know the whole story. *[Give one example of hard work or sacrifice or daily effort or outstanding achievement.]*

"And that's just one example . . . I could go on and on, but we're paying for the banquet hall by the hour. *[If not in a banquet hall]* . . . but we don't have enough food to last us two weeks.

"We haven't even touched on what it's like to be *[name]*'s friend. She is a caring, loyal friend, always there when she is needed, always someone you can count on. But that's only one reason I'm proud to be her friend. I'm proud to be the friend of a woman who has accomplished what we're honoring her for tonight, a person who has done what she has done, who is the kind of all-around person *[name]* is.

"And that's why I raise my glass in a salute to *[name]* as I wish her the fulfillment of all her dreams and wishes, much success and happiness in the years ahead, and of course good health always.

"Here's to you, a great woman, a great citizen, a great friend . . . *[name]*!"